Air Fryer Cookbook

for Beginners

New Healthy, Easy & Low-Carb Recipes 2020#. The most wanted Air Fryer Recipes for A Healthy Weight Loss (with Keto and Vegan Keto Options). Fry, Bake, Grill & Roast.

Dr AMY VOGEL FUNG

Licence to use the book

You must not in any circumstances:

(a)   publish, republish, sell, license, sub-license, rent, transfer, broadcast, distribute or redistribute the book or any part of the book;

(b)   edit, modify, adapt or alter the book or any part of the book;

(c)   use the book or any part of the book in any way that is unlawful or in breach of any person's legal rights under any applicable law, or in any way that is offensive, indecent, discriminatory or otherwise objectionable;

(d)   use the book or any part of the book to compete with us, whether directly or indirectly]

(e)   use the book or any part of the book for a commercial purpose.

You must retain, and must not delete, obscure or remove, all copyright notices and other proprietary notices in the book. The rights granted to you by this disclaimer are personal to you, and you must not permit any third party to exercise these rights. If you breach this disclaimer, then the licence set out above will be automatically terminated upon such breach (whether or not we notify you of termination).

Upon the termination of the licence, you will promptly and irrevocably delete from your computer systems and other electronic devices any copies of the book in your possession or control and will permanently destroy any paper or other copies of the book in your possession or control.

Disclaimer

The information provided in this book is designed to provide helpful information on the subjects discussed and content herein are provided for educational and entertainment purposes only.

The content and information contained in this book have been compiled from sources deemed reliable, and it is accurate to the best of the Author's knowledge, information, and belief.

Although the author and publisher have made every effort to ensure that the information in this book was correct at press time, without any errors and/or omissions, the author and publisher do not assume and hereby disclaim any liability to any party for any loss, damage, or disruption caused by errors or omissions, whether such errors or omission results from negligence, accident, or any other cause.

Further, changes are periodically made to this book as and when needed. Any liability, in terms of inattention or otherwise, by any usage or abuse of any policies, processes, or directions contained within is the solitary and utter responsibility of the recipient reader.

Under no circumstances will any legal responsibility or blame be held against the publisher for any reparation, damages, or monetary loss due to the information herein, either directly or indirectly. You agree that by continuing to read this book, where appropriate and/or necessary, you shall consult a professional (including but not limited to your doctor, attorney, or financial advisor or such other advisor as needed) before using any of the suggested remedies, techniques, or information in this book.

The information contained in this book and its contents is not meant to be used, nor should it be used, to diagnose or treat any medical condition and is not designed to replace or take the place of any form of medical, financial, legal or other professional advice or services, as may be required. Nothing in shared in this book is intended to be any kind of advice. The reader is responsible for his or her own actions and agrees to accept all risks of using the information presented inside this book.

Table of Content

Introduction

You've made the best first step to reducing your meal preparation time by purchasing the Air Fryer Cookbook. You can locate your favorite recipes and whip up a remarkable meal at home in half of the time. All you need to do is 'punch in' the temperature and times. That is only the beginning of your journey with your new Air Fryer recipes. You'll be glad you are beginning a new way of cooking:

- It won't be necessary to add oil to the cooker if you have frozen products that are meant for baking. You only need to adjust the timer and cook. All of the excess fat will drip away into a tray beneath the basket.

- You can cook whatever meat you enjoy and receive delicious and healthy results. You will understand this once you begin trying out some of these new recipes.

- For example, you can cook French fries with a tablespoon of oil versus a vat of oil.

- You only need to remove the cooking bowl, drip pan, or the cooking basket. It is inside a cover, which means you won't have oil vapor deposits on the walls, floors, or countertops.

- You can use the dishwasher to clean the movable parts. You can also use a sponge to clean the bits of food that might be stuck to the AF surfaces.

- It is possible to splurge on the more expensive oils since you only use such a minimal amount.

- The Air Fryer is capable of functioning like so many products, whether you need an oven, a hot grill, a toaster, a skillet, or a deep fryer—it is your answer!

- The machine will automatically shut down when the cooking time is completed. You will have less burned or overheated food items. The fryer will not slip because of the non-slip feet, which help eliminate the risk of the machine from falling off of the countertop. The closed cooking system helps prevent burns from hot oil or other foods.

What is an Air Fryer? How it works? Advantages & Disadvantages.

What is an Air Fryer? Ask any diet conscious person and I bet they'll enthusiastically explain you all details about this virtuous kitchen appliance. Undoubtedly, an

Air fryer is the only kitchen appliance that lets you binge on your favorite snacks while still keeping your overall calorie intake considerably down.

An air fryer is a kitchen appliance that cooks food by circulating super-hot air around the food giving it that beautiful crunch without actually using oil for frying. The crunchy layer which we just mentioned that adheres the surface of any deep fried food, is due to the 'Maillard effect'. General methods of cooking induce the Maillard effect by completely or partially submerging the food in hot oil. Contrasting to which, an air fryer induces the same effect by circulating very hot air (up to 200°C) around the food with the help of a mechanical fan. Very little to mere spraying of oil can still be used to get the traditional essence of any food. Moreover all the cooking units of an air fryer are lined with a non-stick coating. So, even without oil, everything is just fine.

Most air fryers come with adjustable temperature and timer knobs for convenient and customized cooking.

Who doesn't like French Fries but everyone knows the amount of oil it has. Also health conscious people tend to keep a distance from any oily food. But if I tell you that you can have all the Fried food yet keep your oil meter in check sounds fishy? Not in the 21st century, Behold the power of Air Fryer. The Air fryer can reduce oil usage by more than 75%. You can also use no oil if you want to and yet the food tastes great. So, have your fries, chips, chicken wings and still stay well within your daily calorie goals.

Components of an Air fryer

Any air fryer has the following detachable parts:

- Cover (main body).

- Basket holder.

- Divider.

- Basket.

The base of the appliance is the cover or the main body which has the actual functioning unit. Above which there's the basket holder which holds the cooking basket. It has the mechanical fan installed beneath it (this may vary with brands).

Up furthermore, there is the cooking basket where the food is supposed to be kept for cooking. The cooking basket has a base in the form of a wire mesh which allows proper circulation of hot air around the food. Adding to the benefits, the device also has a divider which enables you to cook different varieties of food in the same slot at the exact same time

Why You Should Use an Air Fryer

An air fryer can pretty much do it all. And by all, we mean fry, grill, bake, and roast.

Equipped with sturdy plastic and metal material, the air fryer has many great benefits to offer.

Air Fryers have the ability to:

- Cook multiple dishes at once

- Cut back on fatty oils

- Prepare a meal within minutes

- While every appliance has its cons, the air fryer doesn't offer many.

The fryer may be bulky in weight, but its dimensions are slimmer than most fryers. An air fryer can barely take up any counter space.

If you need fast, healthy, convenient and tasty, then once again, an air fryer may be for you.

No Grease, No Mess

With an air fryer you can enjoy the fact that no oil is needed to cook your food.

All ingredients are cooked with hot air, and offer you the same great look and taste as oiled fried foods.

The best part about not using oil is avoiding those greasy stains on your plates and fingers.

While a little oil can be used with an air fryer, it is not common.

When you do use oil, it is best to apply it directly to the food instead of filling the pan with a puddle of oil, since this may damage the air fryer.

Many people enjoy the idea of eating a healthier version of normally fattening foods. Think of it like this: No oil means no mess and less fat.

Should you decide to prepare your dish with oil, make sure you use it with homemade foods instead of pre-heated foods. Your appliance's manual should include details of which type of oils can be used with the fryer.

Air Fryer Healthier

The biggest quality the air fryer offers is healthier dishes

In comparison to other fryers, air fryers were designed to specifically function without fattening oils and to produce food with up to 80 percent less fat than food cooked with other fryers.

The air fryer can help you lose the weight, you've been dying to get rid of. While it can be difficult to let go of your favorite fried foods, an air fryer will let you have your cake and eat it too.

You can still have your fried dishes, but at the same time, still conserve those calories and saturated fat. The air fryer can also grill, bake and roast foods as well. Offering you an all in one combination, the air fryer is the perfect appliance for anyone looking to switch to a healthier lifestyle.

Fast and Quick

If you're on a tight schedule, you may want to use an air fryer.

Within minutes you can have crunchy golden fries or crispy chicken tenders.

This fryer is perfect for people who are constantly on the go and do not have much time to prepare meals.

With most air fryers, french fries can be prepared within 12 minutes.

That cuts the time you spend in the kitchen by a tremendous amount.

Features

Temperature and Timer

Avoid the waiting time for your fryer to decide when it wants to heat up.

With an air fryer, once you power it on, the fryer will instantly heat.

When using the appliance cold, that is, right after it has been off for a while (since last use) all you have to do is add three minutes to your cooking time to allow for it to heat up properly.

The appliance is equipped with an adjustable temperature control that allows you to set the temperature that can be altered for each of your meals.

Most fryers can go up all the way up to 200-300 degrees.

Because the fryer can cook food at record times, it comes with a timer that can be pre-set with no more than 30 minutes.

You can even check on the progress of your foods without messing up the set time. Simply pull out the pan, and the fryer will pause heating. When you replace the pan, heating will resume.

When your meal is prepared and your timer runs out, the fryer will alert you with its ready sound indicator. But just in-case you can't make it to the fryer when the timer goes, the fryer will automatically switch off to help prevent your ingredients from overcooking and burning.

Food Separator

Some air fryers are supplied with a food separator that enables you to prepare multiple meals at once.

For example, if you wanted to prepare frozen chicken nuggets and french fries, you could use the separator to cook both ingredients at the same time, all the while avoiding the worry of the flavors mixing.

An air fryer is perfect for quick and easy, lunch and dinner combinations. It is recommended to pair similar ingredients together when using the separator.

This will allow both foods to share a similar temperature setting.

Air Filter

Some air fryers are built with an integrated air filter that eliminates those unwanted vapors and food odors from spreading around your house.

No more smelling like your favorite fried foods, the air filter will diffuse that hot oil steam that floats and sticks. You can now enjoy your fresh kitchen smell before, during and after using your air fryer.

Cleaning

No need to fret after using an air fryer, it was designed for hassle-free cleaning.

The parts of the fryer are constructed of non-stick material.

This prevents any food from sticking to surfaces that ultimately make it hard to clean.

It is recommended to soak the parts of the appliances before cleaning.

All parts such as the grill, pan and basket are removable and dishwasher friendly.

After your ingredients are cooked to perfection, you can simply place your parts in the dishwasher for a quick and easy clean.

Tips on cleaning an air fryer:

- Use detergent that specializes in dissolving oil.

- For a maximum and quick cleaning, leave the pan to soak in water and detergent for a few minutes.

- Avoid using metal utensils when cleaning the appliance to prevent scuffs and scratches on the material.

- Always let the fryer cool off for about 30 minutes before you wash it.

Cost Effective

For all that they can do, air fryers can definitely be worth the cost.

It has been highly questionable if the benefits of an air fryer are worth the expense. When you weigh your pros and cons, the air fryer surely leads with its pros. There aren't many fryers on the market that can fry, bake, grill and roast; and also promise you healthier meals.

An air fryer saves you time, and could potentially save you money. Whether the air fryer is cost effective for your life, is ultimately up to you.

Advantages of Air Fryer

In a nutshell, traditional deep fried cooking imparts the food with excessive unnecessary calories by oil absorption during the cooking process. Alternatively, an Air fryer avoids all those extra calories in the form of absorbed oil and produces healthier versions of the same food keeping all the flavours intact.

If you are a food lover, and cannot compromise on the taste and that satisfying deep fried crunch but also want to keep a check on your calorie intake, you should definitely invest in a good air fryer. An air fryer will bless your life with the perfect balance of binge and health.

- Low caloric content food due to very low oil content

- Easy and simple to use

- Easy to clean

- No mess

Disadvantages of Air Fryer

Air fryers have invaded the kitchen appliance industry with a storm owing to the promising claims associated with them. Although air fryers add a great deal of convenience, there are a few limitations to them as well.

1. Not for big families

Air fryers have a limited basket capacity. So, cooking in an Air fryer for more than a few adults in one batch can be a tricky job. However, Air fryers with increased cooking capacities are being introduced to rectify this con.

2. Longer cooking durations

Air fryers exhibit considerably longer cooking times as compared to traditional deep frying methods. To be precise, an Air fryer can take as much as two times the duration when compared to deep fryers.

3. Expensive

Owing to the health benefits associated with Air fryers, some models are priced way more than regular deep fryers. For context, you can get a deep fryer for as less as $50 while an Air fryer averages at around $100.

4. Bulky

As newer Air fryer models with increased cooking capacities are introduced, their overall size has considerably increased. Such bulky models eat way too much of counter space which can be an issue for small kitchens.

Well the disadvantages are being reduced with new iterations and new menus being added to the advantages, it is one of most preferred Home or Kitchen appliances.

How do Air Fryers Work?

An Air Fryer is essentially a small, turbo-powered convection oven for your kitchen counter. It speedily circulates hot air around food to cook it quickly. While the air fryer has a removable basket like a deep fryer, instead of submerging the food into hot oil, the items in the basket are baked by the heat from air flowing around them. (It's the same method as the convection option on a full-size oven or large toaster oven, just miniaturized.)

As a professional recipe developer and food writer, I'm not afraid of deep frying. But, I do appreciate any technique that lets me eat healthier versions of satisfying foods.

Air fryers work by circulating hot air around a food item to create the same crispiness as in traditional fried foods.

Air fryers accomplish this by removing high-fat and high-calorie oils from the cooking process.

By using just 1 tablespoon of cooking oil rather than multiple cups, a person can produce similar results as they would with a deep fryer with a fraction of the fat and calories.

Researchers state that air fryers use heated air that contains fine oil droplets to take the moisture out of the foods. The result is a product that has similar characteristics to fried foods, though with significantly lower levels of fat.

Like many other cooking methods, air-frying triggers a chemical reaction the Maillard effect that improves the color and flavor of air-fried food.

Benefits of Air Fryers

When used properly, Air Fryers offer many healthful benefits:

I.   Using air fryers can promote weight loss

II.   A higher intake of fried foods has direct links with higher obesity risk. This is because deep fried foods tend to be high in fat and calories.

III.   Switching from deep-fried foods to air-fried foods and reducing regular intake of unhealthful oils can promote weight loss.

IV.   Air fryers can be safer than deep fryers

V.   Deep-frying foods involves heating a large container full of scalding oil. This can pose a safety risk. While air fryers do get hot, there is no risk of spilling, splashing, or accidentally touching hot oil. People should use frying machines carefully and follow instructions to ensure safety.

VI.   Air fryers reduce the risk of toxic acrylamide formation

VII. Frying food in oil can cause dangerous compounds to develop, such as acrylamide. This compound forms in certain foods during high-heat cooking methods, such as deep frying.

VIII. By switching to air frying, people can lower the risk of having acrylamide in their food.

IX. Cutting down on deep-fried foods reduces disease risk

Some Adverse Effects of Air Fryers

While Air Fryers have their benefits, they also have their own unique collection of adverse effects, including but not limited to the following:

I.   Air frying does not guarantee a healthful diet

II.   A person should limit their fried food intake rather than replace deep-fried foods with air fried foods.

III.   While air fryers are capable of providing more healthful food options than deep fryers, limiting fried food intake altogether can significantly benefit a person's health.

IV.   Just replacing all deep-fried foods with air-fried foods in no way guarantees a healthful diet.

V.   For optimal health, people should focus on a diet filled with vegetables, fruits, whole grains, and lean protein.

VI.   Air frying can create other harmful compounds

VII. While air fryers reduce the likelihood of acrylamide formation, other potentially harmful compounds could still form.

VIII. Not only does air frying still run the risk of creating acrylamides, but polycyclic aromatic hydrocarbons and heterocyclic amines can result from all high-heat cooking with meat.

IX.   These compounds have associations with cancer risk, according to the National Cancer Institute.

X.   Scientists need to do additional research to clarify exactly how air frying and these compounds correlate.

XI.   Air fried food is not guaranteed to be healthful

XII. Air fryers are capable of making foods that are healthier than deep-fried food, but keep in mind that fried food is still fried food. When cooking excessively with oil, there will always be associated health effects.

Air Fryer FAQs...

Is Air Fried food healthy?

Air frying is healthier than deep frying because you need much less (or no) oil. It is similar in healthiness to conventional ovens, though it's much quicker cooking.

Do Air Fryers need oil?

Nope! Air fryers work by circulating hot air, which makes your food crispy without the need for oil. If you do add oil, it should be directly on the food (for example, rubbed onto vegetables before air frying).

Why does my Air Fryer smoke?

The bottom of your baking pan may be oily. Simply clean it out to prevent the oil from smoking. I also like to place my air fryer under the stove hood so I can fan away the smell of cooking food.

Tips for Usage:

- Allow at least three minutes warm-up time each time you use the fryer so it can reach its correct starting temperature.

- Cooking sprays are an excellent choice to spray on your food before cooking. You can also spray the mesh of the cooking basket to keep anything from sticking to its surface.

- It is essential to pat food items dry if you have marinated or soaked them in to help eliminate splattering or excessive smoke.

- While cooking smaller items such as fries or wings, you can make sure they are cooking evenly by shaking the basket several times during the cooking process.

- If you use aluminum foil or parchment paper, leave a one-half-inch space around the bottom edge of the basket.

- When it comes time to clean the cooking basket, loosen any food particles remaining attached to the basket. Soak each of the attachments in a soapy water solution before scrubbing or placing it in the dishwasher.

Chapter 1: Brunch Specialties

Air Fryer Bacon

Servings Provided: 6

Ingredients Needed:

- Bacon (6 slices)

Preparation Technique:

1. Place the bacon in the bottom of the Air Fryer basket (3.5 quart Air Fryer = 6 strips of bacon).
2. Place a wire rack over the bacon that came with fryer (optional).
3. Air-fry at 350° Fahrenheit for seven to nine minutes. Open the fryer and flip the bacon.
4. Put the Air Fryer basket back in and cook for another 3 minutes or until it's crispy.

Air Fryer Bagels

Servings Provided: 4

Ingredients Needed:

- Self-rising flour (1 cup)
- Zero fat plain Greek yogurt (1 cup)
- Egg (1 for the egg wash)
- Desired garnishes: Sesame or poppy seeds

Preparation Technique:

1. Set the Air Fryer at 330° Fahrenheit ahead of baking time.
2. Whisk the yogurt and flour to form a tacky dough.
3. Dust a preparation surface and roll the dough into a ball, slicing it into four sections.
4. Roll each one into bagel shapes and pinch to close.

5. Prepare two at a time, brushing the tops with egg wash.
6. Set the timer for ten minutes after arranging the bagels in the cooker.
7. For the toppings, brush with a portion of melted butter and season as desired.

Apple Dumplings

Servings Provided: 2

Ingredients Needed:

- Raisins (2 tbsp.)
- Small apples (2)
- Brown sugar (1 tbsp.)
- Puff pastry (2 sheets)
- Melted butter (2 tbsp.)

Preparation Technique:

1. Warm the Air Fryer to reach 356° Fahrenheit.
2. Peel and core the apples. Combine the raisins and sugar. Place the apples on the pastry sheets and fill with the raisin mixture.
3. Fold the pastry over to cover the fixings. Place them on a piece of foil so they won't fall through the fryer. Brush them with melted butter.
4. Air-fry until they're golden brown (25 minutes).
5. *Note*: It's best to prepare using tiny apples.

Avocado Egg Boats

Servings Provided: 2

Ingredients Needed:

- Avocado (1)
- Large eggs (2)
- *Optional Garnishes*:
- Freshly chopped chives
- Parsley
- Pepper
- Salt

Preparation Technique:

1. Set the Air Fryer temperature setting at 350º Fahrenheit.
2. Discard the pit from the avocado. Slice and scoop out part of the flesh and add the seasonings.
3. Break an egg into each half and place it in the Air Fryer. Set the timer for six minutes.
4. Serve using toppings of your choice.

Baked Apple & Walnuts

Servings Provided: 2

Ingredients Needed:

- Apple or pear (1 medium)
- Chopped walnuts (2 tbsp.)
- Raisins (2 tbsp.)

- Light margarine (1.5 tsp. - melted)
- Cinnamon (.25 tsp.)
- Nutmeg (.25 tsp.)
- Water (.25 cup)

Preparation Technique:

1. Set the Air Fryer temperature at 350° Fahrenheit.
2. Cut the apple/pear in half around the middle and spoon out some of the flesh.
3. Place the apple or pear in the pan (to fit in the Air Fryer).
4. In a small mixing container, combine the cinnamon, nutmeg, margarine, raisins, and walnuts.
5. Add the mixture into the centers of the fruit halves.
6. Pour water into the pan.
7. Air-fry for 20 minutes.

Baked Eggs In A Bread Bowl

Servings Provided: 4

Ingredients Needed:

- Large eggs (4)
- Crusty dinner rolls (4)
- Heavy cream (4 tbsp.)
- Mixed herbs - ex. Chopped tarragon, chives, parsley, etc. (4 tbsp. each)
- Grated parmesan cheese (to your liking)

Preparation Technique:

1. Set the Air Fryer at 350º Fahrenheit.
2. Use a sharp knife to remove the top of each of the rolls – setting them aside for later. Use a glass or cookie cutter to make a hole in the bread large enough for the egg.
3. Place the rolls in the fryer basket. Break an egg into the roll and top with the cream and herbs. Sprinkle using a portion of the parmesan.
4. Bake for about 20-25 minutes until the egg is set. The bread should be toasted.
5. After 20 minutes, arrange the tops of the bread on the egg and bake a few more minutes to finish the browning process.
6. Remove from the Air Fryer and wait for five minutes. Serve warm.

Banana Fritters

Servings Provided: 8

Ingredients Needed:

- Vegetable oil (3 tbsp.)
- Breadcrumbs (.75 cup)
- Corn flour (3 tbsp.)
- Ripe peeled bananas (8)
- Egg white (1)

Preparation Technique:

1. Warm the Air Fryer to reach 356° Fahrenheit.

2. Use the low-heat temperature setting to warm a skillet. Pour in the oil and toss in the breadcrumbs. Cook until golden brown.
3. Coat the bananas with the flour. Dip them into the whisked egg white and cover with the breadcrumbs.
4. Arrange the prepared bananas in a single layer of the basket and place the fritter cakes onto a bunch of paper towels to drain before serving.

Cheesy Mushroom Onion Frittata

Servings Provided: 2

Ingredients Needed:

- Olive oil (1 tbsp.)
- Mushrooms (2 cups)
- Onion (1 small)
- Eggs (3)
- Grated cheese (50 g or .5 cup)
- Salt (1 pinch)
- *Also Needed*: 1 Skillet

Preparation Technique:

1. Warm the Air Fryer at 320° Fahrenheit.
2. Prepare a skillet (medium heat) and pour in the oil.
3. Chop the mushrooms and onions. Toss into the pan and sauté for about five minutes before adding them to the Air Fryer.
4. Whisk the eggs and salt. Dump it into the fryer with a sprinkle of cheese.

5. Set the timer for 10 minutes and remove to
   serve.

Chicken Breakfast Burrito

Servings Provided: 1-2

Ingredients Needed:

- Eggs (2)
- Chicken or turkey breast (3-4 slices)
- Avocado (.25 of 1)
- Bell pepper (.25 of 1)
- Mozzarella cheese (.125 cup - grated)
- Pepper and salt (1 pinch each)
- Salsa (2 tbsp.)
- Tortilla (1)

Preparation Technique:

1. Heat the fryer to reach 392º Fahrenheit.
2. Slice the bell pepper and avocado; and set
   aside. In a small mixing container, whisk the
   eggs, pepper, and salt.
3. Fold the fixings into a small pan and arrange it
   in the Air Fryer basket.
4. Set the timer for 5 minutes.
5. When done, transfer the egg from the pan, add
   the fixings, and load the tortilla. Combine all of
   the fixings and wrap it.
6. Add a piece of foil to the Air Fryer tray and add
   the burrito. Heat for three minutes at 356º
   Fahrenheit.

7. Garnish as desired and serve.

Chocolate & Avocado Muffins

Servings Provided: 7

Ingredients Needed:

- Apple cider vinegar (1 tsp.)
- Almond flour (1 cup)
- Baking soda (.5 tsp.)
- Stevia powder (3 scoops)
- Egg (1)
- Melted dark chocolate (1 oz.)
- Butter (4 tbsp.)
- Pitted avocado (.5 cup)

Preparation Technique:

1. Heat the Air Fryer at 355° Fahrenheit.
2. Whisk the baking soda, almond flour, and the vinegar. Melt and add in the chocolate and stevia powder.
3. Whisk the egg in another bowl and add to the mixture along with the butter.
4. Peel, cube, and mash the avocado and add. Blend using a hand mixer until smooth. Pour into the muffin forms (halfway full). Cook them for nine minutes.
5. Reduce the heat (340° Fahrenheit) and cook for another nine minutes.
6. Chill before serving for the best results.

Churros

Servings Provided: 6

Ingredients Needed:

- Butter (.25 cup)
- Milk (.5 cup)
- Salt (1 pinch salt)
- All-purpose flour (.5 cup)
- Eggs (2)
- White sugar (.25 cup)
- Ground cinnamon (.5 tsp.)

Preparation Technique:

1. Heat the Air Fryer at 340º Fahrenheit.
2. Melt the butter in a saucepan using the med-high heat setting. Pour in milk and add salt. Lower heat to medium and let it boil, continuously stirring with a wooden spoon.
3. Quickly add flour all at once. Keep stirring until the dough comes together.
4. Remove from the heat and cool it for 5-7 minutes. Mix in eggs with a wooden spoon until the choux pastry comes together.
5. Spoon the dough into a pastry bag that is fitted with a large star tip. Pipe the dough into strips straight into the Air Fryer basket.
6. Air-fry the churros a for five minutes.
7. In a small mixing container, whisk the cinnamon and sugar (shallow is best).
8. Remove the fried churros from fryer and roll in the cinnamon-sugar mixture.

Delicious Doughnuts In A Jiffy

Servings Provided: 4

Ingredients Needed:

- Flaky jumbo refrigerated dough biscuits (1 can)
- Ground cinnamon (1.5 tsp.)
- White granulated sugar (.5 cup)
- Coconut oil or ghee (as needed)

Preparation Technique:

1. Prepare the fryer to 350º Fahrenheit.
2. Arrange the biscuits on a cutting board. Use a one-inch biscuit cutter to remove the centers.
3. Grease the basket with the oil/ghee.
4. Whisk the sugar and cinnamon.
5. Air-fry for five to six minutes. Fry the holes for three to four minutes.
6. Transfer to a dish and brush using the butter, garnishing using a sprinkle of the cinnamon/sugar mixture.

Tasty Variations:

Glazed: Combine 2-3 tablespoons of milk, 1 cup of powdered sugar, and ½ t. of vanilla. Drizzle in the milk until it reaches a thick paste consistency.

Orange Glazed: Replace the milk with orange juice

along with a bit of orange zest.

Delicious Deep Flavor: Add a sprinkle of pepper to the sugar and cinnamon mixture.

French Toast Soldiers

Servings Provided: 2

Ingredients Needed:

- Wholemeal bread (4 slices)
- Large eggs (2)
- Whole milk (.25 cup)
- Brown sugar (.25 cup)
- Honey (1 tbsp.)
- Cinnamon (1 tsp.)
- Nutmeg (1 pinch)
- Icing sugar (1 pinch)

Preparation Technique:

1. Chop the bread slices into "soldiers." Each slice should make four soldiers.
2. Combine and mix the rest of the fixings (apart from the icing sugar) into a mixing bowl.
3. Dip each one into the mixture. You'll have 16 pieces.
4. Place them on 320º Fahrenheit for 10 minutes or until they're crispy like toast. Halfway through cooking, flip them over so that both sides of the soldiers will be evenly cooked.

5. Garnish using fresh berries and a dusting of icing sugar.

Ham - Egg - Mushroom & Cheese Croissant

Servings Provided: 1

Ingredients Needed:

- Egg (1)
- Mozzarella or cheddar cheese (1.8 oz.)
- Honey shaved ham (3 slices)
- Croissant (1)
- Halved cherry tomatoes (4)
- Small quartered button mushrooms (4)
- *Optional*: Roughly chopped rosemary sprig (half of 1)

Preparation Technique:

1. Help prevent the batter from sticking by lightly greasing the baking dish.
2. Set the Air Fryer temperature to reach 320º Fahrenheit.
3. Measure and add half of the cheese in the bottom of the dish. Add the sliced ham. Leave a space in the center portion of the ham. Break and add the egg with a sprinkle of the rosemary, salt, and pepper.
4. Sprinkle with the last of the cheese.
5. Arrange in the basket and air-fry for eight minutes.

6. Air fry the croissant for about four minutes.
   Serve when the egg is set.

Ham Hash

Servings Provided: 3

Ingredients Needed:

- Ham (10 oz.)
- Parmesan (5 oz.)
- Onion (.5 of 1)
- Butter (1 tbsp.)
- Egg (1)
- Black pepper (1 tsp.)
- Paprika (1 tsp.)
- *Also Needed*: 3 ramekins

Preparation Technique:

1. Set the Air Fryer at 350° Fahrenheit.
2. Peel and dice the onion. Shred the parmesan cheese and slice the ham into small strips.
3. Whisk and mix in the egg, salt, pepper, and paprika.
4. Combine all of the fixings and add to the ramekins with a sprinkle of parmesan.
5. Air Fryer for 10 minutes.
6. Transfer to your plate, and lightly scramble to serve.

Loaded Hash Browns

Servings Provided: 4

Ingredients Needed:

- Russet potatoes (3)
- Red & green peppers (.25 cup each)
- Onions (.25 cup)
- Garlic (2 cloves)
- Paprika (1 tsp.)
- Olive oil (2 tsp.)
- Salt & pepper (as desired)

Preparation Technique:

1. Warm the Air Fryer at 400° Fahrenheit,
2. Prep the fixings. Chop the onions, garlic, and peppers. Use the biggest holes of a cheese grater to prepare the potatoes.
3. Toss into a bowl of cold water to remove the starchiness and make them crunchy (20-25 min.).
4. Drain the water and dry in a towel. Place in a bowl and mix with the fixings. Toss them into the Air Fryer for 10 minutes.
5. Chill slightly before serving.

Pepperoni - Egg & Cheese Pizza

Servings Provided: 1

Ingredients Needed:

- Oregano (.5 tsp.)
- Basil (.5 tsp.)
- Eggs (2)
- Shredded mozzarella cheese (2 tbsp.)
- Thinly sliced pepperoni (4 pieces)
- Also Needed: 1 ramekin

Preparation Technique:

1. Whisk the eggs, basil, and oregano.
2. Pour the eggs into the ramekin, and add the pepperoni and cheese.
3. Arrange the ramekin in the Air Fryer for three minutes and serve.

Quick & Easy Poached Eggs

Servings Provided: 1

Ingredients Needed:

- Boiling water (3 cups)
- Large egg (1)

Preparation Technique:

1. Set the Air Fryer at 390º Fahrenheit.
2. Pour boiling water into the Air Fryer basket.

3. Break the egg into a dish and slide it into the water. Set the basket into the fryer.
4. Set the timer for 3 minutes. When ready, scoop the poached egg into a plate using a slotted spoon.
5. Serve with a serving of toast to your liking.

Sausage Patties

Servings Provided: 4

Ingredients Needed:

- Sausage patties (12 oz pkg.)
- Cooking oil spray

Preparation Technique:

1. Warm the Air Fryer at 400º Fahrenheit.
2. Arrange the patties in a single layer, working in batches if needed.
3. Set the timer for five minutes.
4. Flip the sausage over and cook until they reach 160º Fahrenheit on an instant-read thermometer or about three minutes.

Sausage Wraps

Servings Provided: 8

Ingredients Needed:

- Crescent roll dough (1 can - 8-count)
- American cheese (2 slices)
- Heat & Serve Sausages (8)
- Wooden skewers (8)
- Optional for Dipping: BBQ sauce, ketchup or syrup

Preparation Technique:

1. Set the Air Fryer to 380º Fahrenheit.
2. Open the sausages, and separate the rolls.
3. Slice the cheese into quarters, and add the pieces starting on the widest part of the triangle to the tip. Add the sausage.
4. Gather each end and roll-over the sausage and cheese. Pinch each side together. Add these in two batches to the fryer.
5. Cook for 3-4 minutes.
6. Remove from the fryer and add a skewer. Set it out for serving with the desired garnish.

Scrambled Eggs

Servings Provided: 1

Ingredients Needed:

- Butter (for the fryer basket)
- Eggs (2)
- Salt & black pepper (to your liking)
- Optional: Cheese & tomatoes

Preparation Technique:

1. Warm the Air Fryer at 285º Fahrenheit for about five minutes.
2. Melt a small portion of butter, spreading it out evenly.
3. Whisk and dump the eggs and any other desired fixings desired.
4. Open the fryer every few minutes to whisk the eggs.
5. Serve with a serving of toast or have a scrambled egg sandwich.

Sweet Potato Hash

Servings Provided: 6

Ingredients Needed:

- Large sweet potato (2)
- Bacon (2 slices - cut into small pieces)
- Olive oil (2 tbsp.)
- Smoked paprika (1 tbsp.)

- Sea salt (1 tsp.)
- Ground black pepper (1 tsp.)
- Dried dill weed (1 tsp.)

Preparation Technique:

1. Set the Air Fryer at 400º Fahrenheit.
2. Dice the sweet potatoes and combine with the bacon, olive oil, paprika, salt, pepper, and dill in a large bowl.
3. Toss the mixture into the Air Fryer. Air-fry for 12-16 minutes. Check and stir after ten minutes, and then every three minutes until crispy and browned.

Western Omelet

Servings Provided: 4

Ingredients Needed:

- Eggs (5)
- Cream cheese (3 tbsp.)
- Cilantro (1 tsp.)
- Oregano (1 tsp.)
- Shredded parmesan cheese (3 oz.)
- Green pepper (1)
- Yellow diced onion (1.5)
- Olive oil (1 tsp.)
- Butter (1 tsp.)
- *Also Needed*: 1 Skillet

Preparation Technique:

1. Whisk the eggs, cilantro, oregano, and parmesan. Mix in the cream cheese.
2. Set the Air Fryer at 360º Fahrenheit.
3. Pour the eggs into the fryer basket. Set the timer for 10 minutes.
4. Chop the onions and peppers. Pour oil into a skillet using the medium heat temperature setting. Sauté for 8 minutes.
5. When the eggs are done, serve and garnish with the sautéd veggies.

Delicious Bread Options

Bread Rolls With Potato Stuffing

Servings Provided: 4

Ingredients Needed:

- Bread - white part only (8 slices)
- Potatoes (5 large)
- Oil - frying and brushing (2 tbsp.)
- Finely chopped coriander (1 small bunch)
- Seeded and finely chopped green chilies (2)
- Turmeric (.5 tsp.)
- Curry leaf sprigs (2)
- Mustard seeds (.5 tsp.)
- Finely chopped small onions (2)
- Salt (as desired)

Preparation Technique:

1. Set the Air Fryer at 392º Fahrenheit.
2. Remove the edges of the bread. Peel the potatoes and boil. Mash the potatoes using one teaspoon of salt.
3. On the stovetop, prepare a skillet using one teaspoon of oil. Toss in the mustard seeds and onions. When the seeds sputter, continue frying until they become translucent. Toss in the curry and turmeric.
4. Fry the mixture a few seconds and add the mashed potatoes. Mix well and let it cool. Shape

eight portions of dough into an oval shape. Set them aside for now.

5. Wet the bread with water and press it in your palm to remove the excess water. Place the oval potato into the bread and roll it around the potato mixture. Be sure they are completely sealed.
6. Brush the potato rolls with oil and set aside.
7. Set the timer for 12 to 13 minutes. Cook until crispy and browned.

Cheesy Garlic Bread

Servings Provided: 3-4

Ingredients Needed:

- Bread slices - Round or baguette (5 rounds)
- Sun-dried tomato pesto (5 tsp.)
- Garlic cloves (3)
- Melted butter (4 tbsp.)
- Grated Mozzarella cheese (1 cup)
- *Garnish Options*:
- Chili flakes
- Chopped basil leaves
- Oregano

Preparation Technique:

1. Set the Air Fryer to reach 356º Fahrenheit.
2. Slice the bread loaf into five thick slices.
3. Spread the butter, pesto, and cheese over the bread.

4. Put the slices in the Air Fryer for six to eight
   minutes.
5. Garnish with your choice of toppings.
6. *Note*: Round or baguette bread was used for this
   recipe. It's recommended to add the finely
   chopped garlic cloves to the melted butter ahead
   of time for the best results.

Chapter 2: Lunch Favorites

Bourbon Bacon Burger

Servings Provided: 2

Ingredients Needed:

- Bourbon (1 tbsp.)
- Brown sugar (2 tbsp.)
- Maple bacon (3 strips - cut in half)
- Ground beef - 80% lean (.75 lb.)
- Minced onion (1 tbsp.)
- BBQ sauce (2 tbsp.)

- Salt (.5 tsp.)
- Freshly ground black pepper (as desired)
- Colby Jack/Monterey Jack (2 slices)
- Kaiser rolls (2)
- Lettuce and tomato - for serving
- *For the Sauce*:
- BBQ sauce (2 tbsp.)
- Mayonnaise (2 tbsp.)
- Ground paprika (.25 tsp.)
- Freshly cracked black pepper

Preparation Technique:

1. Warm the Air Fryer at 390º Fahrenheit and pour a little water into the bottom of the fryer drawer.
2. Combine the brown sugar and bourbon in a small bowl. Place the bacon strips in the fryer basket and brush with the brown sugar mixture. Air-fry for four minutes.
3. Flip the bacon over, and recoat using more brown sugar and air-fry for another 4 minutes until crispy.
4. Prepare the burgers. Combine the onion, ground beef, barbecue sauce, salt, and pepper in a large bowl. Shape the meat into two burgers.
5. Put the burgers in the Air Fryer basket and air-fry the burgers at 370º Fahrenheit for 15-20 minutes (15 minutes for rare to medium-rare or 20 minutes for well-done). Flip the burgers halfway through the cooking process.
6. Prepare the burger sauce by combining the BBQ sauce, mayonnaise, paprika, and freshly ground black pepper in a bowl.
7. When the burgers are cooked to your liking, top

each patty with a slice of Colby Jack cheese and air-fry for an additional minute, or long enough to melt the cheese. (You might want to pin the cheese slice to the burger with a toothpick to prevent it from blowing off in your air fryer.)

8. Spread the sauce on the inside of the Kaiser rolls, place the burgers on the rolls, top with the bourbon bacon, lettuce, and tomato and serve.

Cheeseburger 'Mini' Sliders

Servings Provided: 3

Ingredients Needed:

- Cheddar cheese (6 slices)
- Ground beef (1 lb.)
- Freshly cracked black pepper and salt (as desired)
- Dinner rolls (6)

Preparation Technique:

1. Warm the Air Fryer ahead of fry time to 390º Fahrenheit.
2. Shape six (2.5-oz.) patties and dust with the pepper and salt
3. Arrange the burgers in the fryer basket and cook for ten minutes.
4. Take them out of the cooker and add the cheese.
5. Return them to the basket for another minute until the cheese melts.

Chicken Fried Rice

Servings Provided: 5-6

Ingredients Needed:

- Packed cooked chicken (1 cup)
- Cold cooked white rice (3 cups)
- Frozen carrots and peas (1 cup)
- Vegetable oil (1 tbsp.)
- Soy sauce (6 tbsp.)
- Diced onion (.5 cup)
- Also Needed: 7 by 2-inch cake pan

Preparation Technique:

1. Set the Air Fryer at 360º Fahrenheit.
2. Cook and dice the chicken. Prepare the rice. Dice the onion.
3. Add the chilled rice, soy sauce, and oil into a mixing bowl. Stir well.
4. Toss in the onion, chicken, peas, and carrots. Combine the fixings in the Air Fryer and fry for 20 minutes.
5. Enjoy as a luncheon treat or serve as a side with your favorite dinner time meal.

Egg Rolls

Servings Provided: 16

Ingredients Needed:

- Frozen corn (2 cups)
- Black beans (15 oz. can)
- Spinach (13.5 oz. can)
- Jalapeno Jack cheese (1.5 cups)
- Sharp cheddar cheese (1 cup)
- Diced green chiles (4 oz. can)
- Green onions (4)
- Scallions/Green onions (1 bunch)
- Salt (1 tsp.)
- Ground cumin (1 tsp.)
- Chili powder (1 tsp.)
- Egg roll wrappers (16 oz. pkg.)

Preparation Technique:

1. Preheat the Air Fryer to 390º Fahrenheit.
2. Do the prep. Drain and rinse the beans. Drain the chiles and spinach. Shred the cheese and slice the onions. Thaw and mix the corn, beans, spinach, both types of cheese, salt, green chiles, green onions, cumin, and chili powder in a large bowl.
3. Lay an egg roll wrapper at an angle. Moisten all four edges with water - lightly. Place about 1/4 cup of the filling in the middle of the wrapper.
4. Fold one corner over filling and tuck in the sides to form a roll. Repeat with remaining

wrappers and mist each egg roll with cooking spray.
5. Arrange the egg rolls in the basket, making sure they are not touching, cooking in batches if necessary.
6. Fry for 8 minutes; flip and cook until skins are crispy (4 min.).

Fried Tortellini

Servings Provided: 6

Ingredients Needed:

- Cheese tortellini (9-oz. pkg.)
- Panko breadcrumbs (1 cup)
- Freshly grated parmesan (.33 cup)
- Dried oregano (1 tsp.)
- Garlic powder (.5 tsp.)
- Crushed red pepper flakes (.5 tsp.)
- Kosher salt & freshly ground black pepper
- All-purpose flour (1 cup)
- Large eggs (2)
- For Serving: Marinara sauce

Preparation Technique:

1. Set the Air Fryer at 370° Fahrenheit.
2. In a large pot of boiling salted water, prepare the tortellini until al dente and drain.
3. Use three shallow dishes for prep. Combine the panko, parmesan, oregano, garlic powder, salt, pepper, and red pepper flakes in one. In

another, beat the eggs, and in the third bowl, add flour.
4. Coat the tortellini in the flour, then dredge in eggs, and panko mixture. Continue until all of the tortellini are coated.
5. Place in the Air Fryer and fry until crispy (10 min.).
6. Serve with the marinara.

Grilled Cheese Sandwiches

Servings Provided: 2

Ingredients Needed:

- Sharp cheddar cheese (.5 cup)
- White bread or brioche (4 slices)
- Melted butter (.25 cup)

Preparation Technique:

1. Set the Air Fryer at 360º Fahrenheit.
2. Butter all slices of bread (both sides). Assemble each sandwich and arrange them in the fryer basket.
3. Prepare for 5-7 minutes and serve immediately for the best taste results.

Hawaiian Pizzas

Servings Provided: 12

Ingredients Needed:

- Thomas' Light Multi-Grain English Muffins (1 pkg.)
- Pizza sauce (1 cup)
- Canadian Bacon (.5 cup)
- Crushed pineapple (.25 cup)
- Shredded mozzarella cheese (1-2 cups)

Preparation Technique:

1. Set the fryer at 355º Fahrenheit.
2. Gently, using your finger, separate the English muffins.
3. Place a sheet of foil inside the Air Fryer, making sure that air is still able to circulate. Spritz it with a non-stick cooking spray.
4. Add the halves of the English muffins to the fryer (as many as can fit neatly).
5. Top each half with sauce, Canadian bacon, and pineapple, and shredded cheese.
6. Air-fry for 5 minutes. It's essential to check them after about 3 minutes to be sure all toppings are still cooking evenly.
7. Remove and serve.

Loaded Twice-Baked Air-Fried Potatoes

Servings Provided: 2

Ingredients Needed:

- Olive oil (1 tsp.)
- Potato (14-16 oz.)
- Bacon bits (3 slices)
- Finely chopped green onion (1 tbsp. + .25 cup)
- Unsalted butter (1 tbsp.)
- Salt (.25 tsp.)
- Black pepper (.125 tsp.)
- Heavy cream (2 tbsp.)

Preparation Technique:

1. Set the temperature to 400° Fahrenheit.
2. Fry the bacon about ten minutes in a skillet - reserving the fat - and chop into ½-inch pieces.
3. Finely chop the onions.
4. Coat the potato with the oil and add it to the Air Fryer basket for 30 minutes. Turn the potato (spritzing with oil if needed), and cook for another 30 minutes. Cool for a minimum of 20 minutes.
5. Slice the potato length-ways. Scoop out the pulp leaving about ¼-inch borders to support the filling.
6. Whisk the scooped potatoes, bacon fat, bacon bits, .25 of a cup of the cheese, 1.5 tsp. of onions, pepper, salt, butter, and cream. Combine well.
7. Scoop the mixture into the prepared skins.

Garnish with the cheese and place them in the
Air Fryer.
8. Set the timer for 20 minutes or until the tops
   are browned.
9. Sprinkle the rest of the onions on top of the
   potato and serve.

Luncheon Tacos

Servings Provided: 12

Ingredients Needed:

- Corn taco shells (12)
- Ground turkey (1 lb.)
- Gluten-free or Regular taco seasoning (1 pkg.)
- Shredded lettuce
- Black beans
- Shredded Mexican Cheese
- Optional Toppings: Tomatoes, Onions, Salsa

Preparation Technique:

1. Set the Air Fryer at 355-360° Fahrenheit. (Some
   Air Fryers have 355° Fahrenheit as an option,
   and others only have 350° Fahrenheit or 360°
   Fahrenheit .)
2. Foil line it and then spray using a non-stick
   cooking spray.
3. Rinse and drain the beans.
4. In a medium-sized skillet, brown the turkey.
   Drain if needed, add in the taco seasoning.

5. Build the taco shell using cooked meat, lettuce, beans, and cheese.
6. Add the tacos to the Air Fryer.
7. Cook for 4 minutes until crispy.
8. Note - If you foil-line the basket of the Air Fryer, be sure not to fully cover the base, as not to impede the airflow.

Mac N Cheese Balls

Servings Provided: 2

Ingredients Needed:

- Macaroni and cheese – leftovers are good (2 cups)
- Shredded cheddar cheese (.33 cup)
- Milk (2 cups)
- Eggs (3)
- White flour (.75 cup)
- Plain breadcrumbs (1 cup)

Preparation Technique:

1. Heat the Air Fryer at 360º Fahrenheit.
2. Combine the leftovers with the shredded cheese.
3. Add the breadcrumbs into a dish.
4. Measure the flour into another bowl.
5. Combine the milk and eggs.
6. Make two balls from the mac n cheese.
7. Roll the balls in the flour, eggs, and lastly the breadcrumbs.
8. Arrange the balls in the fryer basket. Press 'M'

and go to the chicken icon.

9. Set the timer for 10 minutes – rotating halfway through the cooking cycle.

Pigs In A Blanket

Servings Provided: 4

Ingredients Needed:

- Crescent rolls (8 oz. can)
- Cocktail franks (12 oz. pkg.)

Preparation Technique:

1. Warm the Air Fryer at 330º Fahrenheit.
2. Rinse and dry the franks using paper towels.
3. Slice the dough into rectangular strips (1.5 inches x 1-inch).
4. Roll the dough around the franks, but leave the ends open.
5. Place them in the freezer for approximately five minutes.
6. Transfer them to the fryer for 6-8 minutes.
7. Raise the temperature setting to 390º Fahrenheit. Continue cooking for approximately three more minutes.

Pita Bread Pizza - Pepperoni Sausage & Onion

Servings Provided: 1

Ingredients Needed:

- Pizza sauce (1 tbsp.)
- Pita bread (1)
- Mozzarella cheese (.25 cup)
- Olive oil (1 spritz)

Ingredients Needed - The Toppings:

- Pepperoni (7 slices)
- Garlic (.5 tsp.)
- Sausage (.25 cup)
- Onions (1 tbsp.)

Preparation Technique:

1. Warm the Air Fryer to 350º Fahrenheit.
2. Spoon the sauce onto the bread.
3. Mince the garlic. Thinly slice the onions. Toss on the toppings and spritz using a drizzle of oil.
4. Arrange the bread in the Air Fryer and place it on the trivet/rack.
5. Set the timer for six minutes. Serve when it's browned.

Pizza Dogs

Servings Provided: 2

Ingredients Needed:

- Hot dogs (2)
- Pepperoni (4 slices - halved)
- Pizza sauce (.5 cup)
- Hot dog buns (2)
- Mozzarella cheese (.25 cup)
- Sliced olives (2 tsp.)

Preparation Technique:

1. Warm the Air Fryer at 390º Fahrenheit.
2. Make four slits down each hot dog and place them in the Air Fryer basket. Set the timer for 3 minutes. Transfer to a cutting board.
3. Place a pepperoni half in each slit of the hot dogs. Portion the pizza sauce between buns and fill with the hot dogs, mozzarella cheese, and olives.
4. Return the hot dogs back into the fryer basket and cook until buns are crisp and cheese is melted (2 min.).

Portobello Stuffed Mushrooms

Servings Provided: 3

Ingredients Needed:

- Portobello mushrooms (3)
- Minced garlic (1 tsp.)
- Medium diced onion (1)
- Grated mozzarella cheese (3 tbsp.)
- Chopped ham (2 slices)
- Diced tomato (1)
- Diced green pepper (1)
- Sea salt (.5 tsp.)
- Pepper (.25 tsp.)
- Olive oil (1 tbsp.)

Preparation Technique:

1. Heat the Air Fryer temperature setting at 320º Fahrenheit.
2. Rinse, dry, and discard the stems from the mushrooms. Drizzle with oil and set aside for now.
3. Mix the cheese, tomato, onion, pepper, salt, garlic, bell peppers, and ham. Stuff the mixture into the mushroom caps.
4. Arrange the mushrooms in the Air Fryer to cook for eight minutes.
5. Serve with your favorite main dish or for a delicious lunch treat.

Ravioli

Servings Provided: 4-5

Ingredients Needed:

- Olive oil (as needed)
- Cheese or meat ravioli (1 pkg.)
- Marinara sauce (1 jar)
- Buttermilk (1 cup)
- Breadcrumbs - Italian-style (2 cups)
- Parmesan cheese (.25 cup)

Preparation Technique:

1. Set the Air Fryer temperature at 200º Fahrenheit.
2. Add the buttermilk into a dish and dip in the ravioli.
3. Mix a spoonful of oil with the breadcrumbs and coat the ravioli using the breadcrumbs.
4. Arrange the ravioli in the fryer using a layer of parchment baking paper for approximately five minutes.
5. *Note*: It is best to use ready-made ravioli and sauce.

Reuben Roasted Turkey Sandwiches

Servings Provided: 2

Ingredients Needed:

- Rye bread (4 slices)
- Skinless – roasted turkey breast (8 slices)
- Coleslaw (4 tbsp.)
- Swiss cheese (8 slices)
- Salted butter (2 tbsp.)
- Russian dressing (2 tbsp.)

Preparation Technique:

1. Prepare two slices of bread on one side with butter and place them, butter side down, on the cutting board.
2. In layers, arrange the turkey, cheese, coleslaw, and Russian dressing on top of the two slices of bread. Fold them together to make one sandwich.
3. Add the sandwich to the Air Fryer basket.
4. Select the *bake icon* setting (310º Fahrenheit for 12 min.).
5. After 6 minutes, flip the sandwich and continue until browned.
6. Slice and serve.

Roasted Veggie Pasta Salad

Servings Provided: 6

Ingredients Needed:

- Yellow squash (1)
- Brown mushrooms (4 oz.)
- Zucchini (1)
- Red - Green - Orange bell peppers (1 each)
- Red onion (1)
- Freshly cracked black pepper and salt (1 pinch each)
- Italian seasoning (1 tsp.)
- Grape tomatoes (1 cup)
- Pitted Kalamata olives (.5 cup)
- Cooked Rigatoni or Penne Rigate (1 lb.)
- Olive oil (.25 cup)
- Freshly chopped basil (2 tbsp.)
- Balsamic vinegar (3 tbsp.)

Preparation Technique:

1. Set the Air Fryer temperature to 380⁰ Fahrenheit.
2. Cut the peppers into large chunks and slice the red onion. Slice the tomatoes and olives into halves. Cut the squash and zucchini into half-moons.
3. Toss the red onion, mushrooms, peppers, squash, and zucchini in a large mixing container. Drizzle with a spritz of oil, tossing well using the black pepper, salt, and Italian seasoning.
4. Prepare in the Air Fryer until the veggies are softened - not mushy (12 to 15 min.). Toss the

fixings in the basket about halfway through the cooking cycle for even frying.

5. Combine the cooked pasta, roasted veggies, olives, and tomatoes into a large container. Pour in the vinegar, and toss.
6. Keep it refrigerated until ready to serve. Garnish using the fresh basil as serving time.

Simple Hot Dogs & Cheese

Servings Provided: 2

Ingredients Needed:

- Hot dogs (2)
- Hot dog buns (2)
- Grated cheese (2 tbsp.)

Preparation Technique:

1. Heat the Air Fryer for four (4) minutes at 390º Fahrenheit.
2. Arrange the hot dogs in the Air Fryer and cook for five minutes.
3. Place the hot dog on the bun and top it off with cheese.
4. Place in the fryer for about two minutes to melt the cheese and serve.

Weight Watchers Mozzarella Cheese Sticks

Servings Provided: 5

Ingredients Needed:

- Mozzarella string cheese (10 pieces)
- Italian breadcrumbs (1 cup)
- Egg (1)
- Flour (.5 cup)
- Marinara sauce (1 cup)
- Pepper and salt (as desired)

Preparation Technique:

1. Warm the Air Fryer at 400º Fahrenheit.
2. Toss the breadcrumbs, salt, and pepper.
3. Prepare three dishes. Dip each piece of cheese in flour, egg, and lastly the breadcrumbs.
4. Chill the sticks for one hour to help them hold the stick shape during frying.
5. Lightly spritz the sticks with coconut oil using a baking brush.
6. Arrange the prepared sticks in the Air Fryer. Set the timer for 8 minutes. At that point, turn them over using tongs and air-fry for another 8 minutes.
7. Wait for 5 minutes and remove from the pan and serve.

Chapter 3: Seafood & Fish Choices

Black Cod With Fennel, Kale, Pecans & Grapes

Servings Provided: 2

Ingredients Needed:

- Black cod/sablefish (2 fillets/6-8 oz.)
- Olive oil
- Freshly cracked black pepper and salt
- Small fennel bulb (1)
- Grapes (1 cup)
- Shredded kale (3 cups)
- Pecans (.5 cup)
- Olive oil (2 tbsp.)
- White wine vinegar/white balsamic wine (2 tsp.)

Preparation Technique:

1. Warm the Air Fryer to 400º Fahrenheit.
2. Sprinkle the fillets with salt, pepper, and a drizzle of olive oil.
3. Arrange the fish - skin side down- in the basket. Air-fry for ten minutes in the Air Fryer. Remove the fish and add to a dish with foil – loose to vent and rest.
4. Toss the fennel, pecans, and grapes. Provide a drizzle of oil along with a shake of salt and pepper. Add to the basket. Air fry for five minutes – shaking once during the cooking process.
5. Place the kale in a dish. Add the grapes, pecans, and fennel with the olive oil (2 tablespoons) and balsamic vinegar.
6. Serve with a side dish.

Breaded Cod Sticks

Servings Provided: 5

Ingredients Needed:

- Milk (3 tbsp.)
- Large eggs (2)
- Breadcrumbs (2 cups)
- Salt (.25 tsp.)
- Black pepper (.5 tsp.)
- Almond flour (1 cup)
- Cod (1 lb.)

Preparation Technique:

1. Heat the Air Fryer at 350º Fahrenheit.
2. Prepare three bowls; one with the milk and eggs, one with the pepper, salt, and breadcrumbs, and another with almond flour.
3. Dip the sticks in the flour, egg mixture, and breadcrumbs.
4. Place in the basket and set the timer for 12 minutes. Toss the basket halfway through the cooking process.
5. Serve with your favorite sauce.

Cajun Salmon

Servings Provided: 1-2

Ingredients Needed:

- Salmon fillet (1 - 7 oz.) 0.75-inches thick
- Juice (¼ of a lemon)
- Cajun seasoning
- Optional: Sprinkle of sugar

Preparation Technique:

1. Set the Air Fryer at 356º Fahrenheit to preheat for five minutes.
2. Rinse and dry the salmon with a paper towel. Cover the fish with the Cajun coating mix.
3. Place the fillet in the air fryer for seven minutes with the skin side up.
4. Serve with a sprinkle of lemon and dusting of sugar if desired.

Cajun Shrimp

Servings Provided: 4-6

Ingredients Needed:

- Olive oil (1 tbsp.)
- Old Bay seasoning (.5 tsp.)
- Tiger shrimp (1.25 lb. or 16-20)
- Smoked paprika (.25 tsp.)
- Cayenne pepper (.25 tsp.)
- Salt (1 pinch)

Preparation Technique:

1. Heat the Air Fryer to reach 390º Fahrenheit.
2. Coat the shrimp using the oil and spices.
3. Toss the shrimp in the fryer basket and set the timer for five minutes.
4. Serve with your favorite side dish.

Clams Oregano

Servings Provided: 4

Ingredients Needed:

- Shucked clams (24)
- Unseasoned breadcrumbs (1 cup)
- Melted butter (4 tbsp.)
- Garlic cloves (3)
- Dried oregano (1 tsp.)
- Parsley (.25 cup)
- Grated parmesan cheese (.25 cup)
- *For the Pan*: 1 c. sea salt

Preparation Technique:

1. Heat the Air Fryer a few minutes at 400º Fahrenheit.
2. Mince the garlic. Chop the parsley to combine with the breadcrumbs, oregano, parmesan cheese, and melted butter in a medium mixing bowl.
3. Using a heaping tablespoon of the crumb

mixture, and add it to the clams.

4. Fill the insert with the salt, arrange the clams inside, and air-fry for three minutes.
5. Garnish them using lemon wedges and fresh parsley.

Coconut Shrimp

Servings Provided: 3

Ingredients Needed:

- Jumbo raw shrimp (12)
- Cornstarch (1 tbsp.)
- Oil (.5 tbsp.)
- Unsweetened dried coconut (1 cup)
- White all-purpose flour (1 cup)
- Uncooked egg whites (1 cup)
- Panko (1 cup)

Preparation Technique:

1. Rinse and drain the shrimp on a layer of paper towels.
2. Heat the Air Fryer ahead of time to 350º Fahrenheit.
3. In one dish, whisk the cornstarch and oil.
4. Break the egg whites into another container and whisk.
5. Combine the coconut and panko in a mixing container.
6. Cover each shrimp in the cornstarch mix, egg whites, and the coconut mixture.

7. Air-fry for ten minutes. Turn the shrimp over after five minutes for a more even cooking.

Crispy Halibut

Servings Provided: 4

Ingredients Needed:

- Halibut fillets (4)
- Fresh chives (.25 cup)
- Fresh parsley (.5 cup)
- Fresh dill (.25 cup)
- Black pepper & sea salt (to your liking)
- Pork rinds (.75 cup)
- Extra-virgin olive oil (1 tbsp.)
- Finely grated lemon zest (1 tbsp.)

Preparation Technique:

1. Warm the Air Fryer to reach 390º Fahrenheit.
2. Chop the chives, dill, and parsley. Combine all of the dry fixings – parsley, pork rinds, chives, dill, lemon zest, black pepper, sea salt, and olive oil.
3. Rinse the halibut thoroughly and let them drain well on paper towels.
4. Prepare a baking tin to fit in the cooker. Spoon the rinds over the fish and press.

Fish & Chips

Servings Provided: 4

Ingredients Needed:

- Catfish fillets or similar fish (2)
- Wholemeal bread for breadcrumbs (3 slices)
- Medium beaten egg (1)
- Bag tortilla chips (0.88 oz. or approximately/25g)
- Juice and rind of 1 lemon
- Pepper and salt
- Parsley (1 tbsp.)

Preparation Technique:

1. Warm the fryer before baking time to reach 356º Fahrenheit.
2. Zest and juice the lemon.
3. Slice the fillets into four pieces ready for cooking. Season each one with the lemon juice and set aside for a few minutes.
4. Use a food processor to mix the tortillas, parsley, pepper, breadcrumbs, and lemon zest.
5. Whisk the egg and egg wash the fish. Run it through the crumb mixture. Place them onto the baking tray and cook until crispy.
6. Preparation time is ten minutes with a total cooking time of fifteen minutes, so wait patiently to enjoy.

Fried Catfish

Servings Provided: 3

Ingredients Needed:

- Olive oil (1 tbsp.)
- Seasoned fish fry (.25 cup)
- Catfish fillets (4)

Preparation Technique:

1. Heat the Air Fryer to reach 400º Fahrenheit before fry time.
2. Rinse the catfish and pat dry using a paper towel.
3. Dump the seasoning into a sizeable zipper-type bag. Add the fish and shake to cover each fillet. Spray with a spritz of cooking oil spray and add to the basket.
4. Set the timer for 10 minutes. Flip, and reset the timer for ten additional minutes. Turn the fish once more and cook for 2-3 minutes.
5. Once it reaches the desired crispiness, transfer to a plate, and serve.

Ginger Cod Steaks

Servings Provided: 2

Ingredients Needed:

- Large cod steaks (2 slices)
- Turmeric powder (.25 tsp.)

- Ginger powder (.5 tsp.)
- Garlic powder (.5 tsp.)
- Salt & pepper (1 pinch)
- Plum sauce (1 tbsp.)
- Ginger slices (to taste)
- Kentucky Kernel Seasoned Flour (+) Cornflour (1 part of each)

Preparation Technique:

1. Dry off the steaks and marinate using the pepper, salt, ginger powder, and turmeric powder for a few minutes.
2. Lightly coat the steaks with the cornflour/Kentucky mix.
3. Set the temperature in the fryer to 356º Fahrenheit for 15 minutes and increase to 400º Fahrenheit for 5 minutes.
4. Prepare the sauce in a wok. Brown the ginger slices and remove from the heat. Stir in the plum sauce adding water to thin as needed.
5. Serve the steaks with a drizzle of sauce.

Quick & Easy Crab Sticks

Servings Provided: 2-3

Ingredients Needed:

- Crab sticks (1 package)
- Cooking oil spray (as needed)

Preparation Technique:

1. Take each of the sticks out of the package and unroll it until the stick is flat. Tear the sheets into thirds.
2. Arrange them on a baking tray and lightly spritz using cooking spray. Set the timer for 10 minutes.
3. *Note*: If you shred the crab meat, you can cut the time in half, but they will also easily fall through the holes in the basket.

Salmon Patties

Servings Provided: 6-8

Ingredients Needed:

- Salmon portion (1 -7 oz.)
- Large russet potatoes (3 - 14 oz.)
- Frozen veggies (.33 cup)
- Dill sprinkles (2)
- Egg (1)
- *For the Coating*: Breadcrumbs
- Olive oil spray

- Dash of pepper and salt

Preparation Technique:

1. Warm the temperature of the Air Fryer to 356º Fahrenheit.
2. Parboil and drain the veggies. Peel and dice the potatoes into small bits. Boil for about ten minutes. Mash and put them in the fridge to chill.
3. Grill the salmon for 5 minutes, flake it apart and set it aside.
4. Combine all of the fixings and shape into patties.
5. Evenly coat them with breadcrumbs and spray them with a bit of olive spray.
6. Place in the fryer for 10-12 minutes.

Sriracha & Honey Tossed Calamari

Servings Provided: 1-2

Ingredients Needed:

- Calamari tubes - tentacles if you prefer (.5 lb.)
- Club soda (1 cup)
- Four (1 cup)
- Salt - red pepper & black pepper (2 dashes each)
- Honey (.5 cup) + Sriracha (1-2 tbsp.)
- Red pepper flakes (2 shakes)

Preparation Technique:

1. Thoroughly rinse the calamari and blot it dry using a bunch of paper towels. Slice into rings (.25-inch wide). Toss the rings into a bowl. Pour in the club soda and stir until all are submerged. Wait for about ten minutes.
2. Sift the salt, flour, red pepper, and black pepper. Set aside for now.
3. Dredge the calamari through the flour mixture, and place it on a platter until ready to fry.
4. Spritz the basket of the Air Fryer with a small amount of cooking oil spray. Arrange the calamari in the basket, careful not to crowd it too much.
5. Set the temperature at 375º Fahrenheit and the timer for 11 minutes.
6. Shake the basket twice during the cooking process, loosening any rings that may stick.
7. Remove from the basket, toss with the sauce and return to the Air Fryer for two more minutes.
8. Serve with additional sauce as desired.
9. Make the sauce by combining honey, sriracha, and red pepper flakes in a small bowl, mix until combined.

Teriyaki Glazed Halibut Steak

Servings Provided: 3

Ingredients Needed:

- Halibut steak (1 lb.)
- *The Marinade:*
- Low-sodium soy sauce (.66 cup)
- Mirin Japanese cooking wine (.5 cup)
- Sugar (.25 cup)
- Orange juice (.25 cup)
- Lime juice (2 tbsp.)
- Ground ginger (.25 tsp.)
- Crushed red pepper flakes (.25 tsp.)
- Smashed garlic (1 clove)

Preparation Technique:

1. Set the Air Fryer at 390º Fahrenheit.
2. Combine all of the marinade components in a saucepan, bringing it to a boil. Lower the heat setting to medium and cool.
3. Pour half of the marinade in a plastic bag with the halibut and zip it closed. Marinate in the fridge for about 30 minutes.
4. Air-fry the halibut for 10 to 12 minutes. Brush using the remaining glaze over the steak.
5. Serve with a bed of rice. Add a little basil or mint or basil for extra flavoring.

Chapter 4: Poultry Options

BBQ Chicken - Gluten-Free

Servings Provided: 4

Ingredients Needed:

- Boneless - skinless chicken breast (2 large)
- Seasoned flour/Gluten-free seasoned flour (.5 cup)
- Barbecue sauce (1 cup)
- Olive oil cooking spray

Preparation Technique:

1. Heat the Air Fryer to 390º Fahrenheit.
2. Chop the chicken into bite-size chunks and place in a mixing bowl. Coat with the seasoned flour.
3. Lightly spritz the basket of the Air Fryer with olive oil cooking spray and evenly pour the chicken into the cooker.
4. Set the timer for 8 minutes.
5. Open the Air Fryer, coat with olive oil spray, and flip the chicken as needed.
6. Air-fry the chicken for eight more minutes.
7. Be sure its internal reading is at least 165º Fahrenheit.
8. Place the chicken into a dish and add the sauce to cover.
9. Line the Air Fryer with a sheet of foil or add the chicken back to the fryer and cook for another 3 minutes until the sauce is warmed and the chicken is a bit more crispy and coated. Serve.

Buffalo Chicken Wings

Servings Provided: 2-3

Ingredients Needed:

- Chicken wings (5 - approx. 14 oz.)
- Salt & black pepper (as desired)
- Cayenne pepper (2 tsp. or to taste)
- Red hot sauce (2 tbsp.)
- Melted butter (1 tbsp.)
- *Optional*: Garlic powder (.5 tsp.)

Preparation Technique:

1. Heat the Air Fryer temperature to reach 356º Fahrenheit.
2. Slice the wings into three sections (end tip, middle joint, and drumstick). Pat each one thoroughly dry using a paper towel.
3. Combine the pepper, salt, garlic powder, and cayenne pepper on a platter. Lightly cover the wings with the powder.
4. Arrange the chicken onto the wire rack and bake for 15 minutes, turning once at 7 minutes.
5. Combine the hot sauce with the melted butter in a dish to garnish the baked chicken when it is time to be served.

Chicken Breast Tenderloins

Servings Provided: 4

Ingredients Needed:

- Butter/vegetable oil (2 tbsp.)
- Breadcrumbs (3.33 tbsp.)
- Egg (1)
- Chicken tenderloins (8)

Preparation Technique:

1. Heat the Air Fryer temperature to 356º Fahrenheit.
2. Combine the breadcrumbs and oil - stirring until the mixture crumbles.
3. Whisk the egg and dredge the chicken through the egg, shaking off the excess.
4. Dip each piece of chicken into the crumbs and evenly coat.
5. Set the timer for 12 minutes.

Chicken Curry

Servings Provided: 4

Ingredients Needed:

- Chicken breast (1 lb.)
- Olive oil (1 tsp.)
- Onion (1)
- Garlic (2 tsp.)
- Lemongrass (1 tbsp.)

- Chicken stock (.5 cup)
- Apple cider vinegar (1 tbsp.)
- Coconut milk (.5 cup)
- Curry paste (2 tbsp.)

Preparation Technique:

1. Warm the fryer to reach 365º Fahrenheit.
2. Dice the chicken into cubes. Peel and dice the onion and combine in the Air Fryer basket. Cook for five minutes.
3. Remove the basket and add the rest of the fixings. Mix well and air-fry for ten more minutes.
4. Serve for a quick and easy meal.

Chicken Fillet Strips

Servings Provided: 4

Ingredients Needed:

- Chicken fillets (1 lb.)
- Paprika (1 tsp.)
- Heavy cream (1 tbsp.)
- Salt & pepper (.5 tsp.)
- Butter (as needed)

Preparation Technique:

1. Heat the Air Fryer at 365º Fahrenheit.

2. Slice the fillets into strips and dust with salt and pepper.
3. Add a light coating of butter to the basket.
4. Arrange the strips in the basket and air-fry for six minutes.
5. Flip the strips and continue frying for another five minutes.
6. When done, garnish with the cream and paprika. Serve warm.

Chicken Kabobs

Servings Provided: 2

Ingredients Needed:

- Chicken breasts (2)
- Mushrooms (6)
- Bell peppers (3 various colors)
- Honey (.33 cup)
- Soy sauce (.33 cup)
- Salt and pepper (to your liking)
- Sesame seeds

Preparation Technique:

1. Set the temperature of the fryer to 338° Fahrenheit.
2. Slice the mushrooms in half. Dice the peppers and chicken.
3. Coat the chicken with a couple of squirts of oil and a pinch of pepper and salt.
4. Mix the soy and honey. Toss in a few sesame seeds and stir.

5. Arrange the peppers, chicken, and mushroom bits onto a skewer.
6. Cover the kabobs with the sauce and arrange them in the basket of the Air Fryer.
7. Air-fry for 15-20 minutes and serve.

Chicken Pot Pie

Servings Provided: 4

Ingredients Needed:

- Chicken tenders (6)
- Potatoes (2)
- Condensed cream of celery soup (1.5 cups)
- Heavy cream (.75 cup)
- Thyme (1 sprig)
- Dried bay leaf (1 whole)
- Refrigerated buttermilk biscuits (5)
- Milk (1 tbsp.)
- Egg yolk (1)

Preparation Technique:

1. Set the Air Fryer at 320º Fahrenheit.
2. Peel and dice the potatoes. Combine all of the fixings in a skillet except for the milk, egg yolk, and biscuits. Bring it to a boil using the medium-heat temperature setting.
3. Empty the mixture into the baking tin. Cover with a sheet of aluminum foil. Prepare a sling using a length of foil to make a handle. Place the pan into the fry basket using the sling and cook

for 15 minutes.

4. After the pie completes the cycle, prepare an egg wash using the milk and egg yolk.
5. Arrange the biscuits onto the baking pan and brush using the egg wash mixture. Set the timer for an additional ten minutes (300º Fahrenheit).
6. Serve when the biscuits are golden brown.

Crispy Chicken Sliders

Servings Provided: 6/12 sliders

Ingredients Needed:

- Tyson Crispy Chicken Strips (1 pkg.)
- Sweet Hawaiian Rolls (1 pkg.)
- *Optional Ingredients*:
- Spinach leaves
- Tomatoes
- Honey mustard

Preparation Technique:

1. Place the six chicken strips in the Air Fryer basket with a coating of olive oil spray. Cook at 390º Fahrenheit for 8 minutes.
2. Slice the rolls in half and top them with honey mustard, spinach, and tomatoes or other toppings of your choice.
3. Slice the chicken strips into chunks and place them on the rolls.

Fried Chicken Thighs

Servings Provided: 2

Ingredients Needed:

- Chicken thighs - no skin (2)
- Fresh parsley (3 sprigs)
- Garlic powder – for dusting
- Lemon (half if 1)
- Fresh rosemary (1-2 sprigs)
- Chili flakes - salt & black pepper (as desired)

Preparation Technique:

1. Rinse the thighs and drain between a few paper towels.
2. Clean the rosemary sprigs and remove the stems. Mince the parsley.
3. Combine the parsley, chili flakes, salt, pepper, garlic powder, rosemary leaves, and lemon juice. Add the thighs and marinate overnight in the fridge.
4. *Warm* the Air Fryer at 356º Fahrenheit. Air-fry for 12 minutes.

Garlic Herb Turkey Breast

Servings Provided: 6

Ingredients Needed:

- Turkey breast (2 lb.)
- Freshly ground black pepper & Kosher salt
- Melted butter (4 tbsp.)
- Garlic (3 cloves)
- Thyme (1 tsp.)
- Rosemary (1 tsp.)

Preparation Technique:

1. Warm the Air Fryer to reach 375° Fahrenheit.
2. Pat the turkey breast dry and season both sides with salt and pepper.
3. Mince the garlic and chop the rosemary and thyme.
4. In a small bowl, combine the melted butter, garlic, thyme, and rosemary. Brush using butter all over turkey breast.
5. Place in the Air Fryer basket, skin side up, and cook for 40 minutes or until internal temperature reaches 160° Fahrenheit, flipping halfway through.
6. Wait for five minutes before slicing.

Mustard-Glazed Turkey Breast

Servings Provided: 6

Ingredients Needed:

- Olive oil (2 tsp.)
- Whole turkey breast (5 lb.)
- Salt (1 tsp.)
- Dried thyme (1 tsp.)
- Butter (1 tsp.)
- Freshly cracked black pepper (.5 tsp.)
- Smoked paprika (.5 tsp.)
- Dried sage (.5 tsp.)
- Maple syrup (.25 tsp.)
- Dijon mustard (2 tbsp.)

Preparation Technique:

1. Warm the fryer to 350º Fahrenheit.
2. Prepare the turkey with a spritz of olive oil.
3. Mix the sage, salt, thyme, pepper, and paprika as a rub. Use it as a coating for the turkey.
4. Arrange the breast in the fryer basket and set the timer for 25 minutes. Rotate it on its side and fry another 12 minutes. It's done when it reaches 165º Fahrenheit – internal temperature.
5. In the meantime, whisk the butter, syrup, and mustard in a saucepan. Turn the breast again and brush using the glaze. Give it a final five minutes until crispy.
6. Cover using a foil tent for five minutes, slice, and serve.

Parmesan Chicken

Servings Provided: 4

Ingredients Needed:

- Chicken breast (2 - about 8 oz. each)
- Seasoned breadcrumbs (6 tbsp.)
- Grated parmesan cheese (2 tbsp.)
- Olive oil/melted butter (1 tbsp.)
- Reduced-fat mozzarella cheese (6 tbsp.)
- Marinara sauce (.5 cup)

Preparation Technique:

1. Set the Air Fryer at 360° Fahrenheit for 3 minutes.
2. Slice the chicken breasts into halves, then into four thin cutlets.
3. Combine the parmesan cheese and breadcrumbs in a bowl.
4. Melt the butter in another dish.
5. Lightly brush the butter onto the chicken, then dip into the breadcrumb mixture.
6. When the Air Fryer is ready, arrange two pieces in the basket and spray the top with a bit of cooking oil.
7. Fry for 6 minutes; turn and top each with one tablespoon of the sauce, and 1.5 tablespoons of shredded mozzarella cheese.
8. Cook until the cheese is melted (3 min.).
9. Set aside and keep warm, repeat with the remaining two pieces.

Philly Chicken Cheese Steak Stromboli

Servings Provided: 2-4

Ingredients Needed:

- Vegetable oil (1 tsp.)
- Onion (half of 1)
- Chicken breasts (2/total of 1 lb.)
- Worcestershire sauce (1 tbsp.)
- Pizza dough (14 oz. pkg. - homemade or store-bought)
- Freshly cracked black pepper & salt
- Cheese Whiz or your favorite cheese sauce (.5 cup)
- Grated Cheddar cheese (1.5 cups)

Preparation Technique:

1. Warm the Cheese Whiz in the microwave.
2. Set the temperature to 400º Fahrenheit in the Air Fryer.
3. Place the onion in the fryer for eight minutes – shaking gently halfway through the cycle. Thinly slice and add the chicken and Worcestershire sauce, salt, and pepper – tossing evenly. Air fry for another eight minutes – stirring several times. Remove and let the mixture cool.
4. Lightly flour a flat surface and press out the dough into a rectangle of 11x13 (the long side facing you). Sprinkle half of the cheddar over the dough. Leave a one-inch border - topping it off with the onion/chicken mixture.
5. Drizzle the warmed cheese sauce over the top,

finishing with the rest of the cheddar cheese.

6. Roll the stromboli toward the empty corner
   (away from you). Keep the filling tight and tuck
   in the ends. Arrange it seam side down and
   shape in a "U" to fit into the basket. Slice four
   slits in the top with the tip of a knife.
7. Lightly brush the top with a little oil. Set the
   temperature to 370º Fahrenheit.
8. Spray the basket and add the stromboli. Fry for
   12 minutes – turning about halfway through the
   cooking process.
9. Use a serving platter and invert the tasty treat
   from the basket. Arrange it on a cutting board
   and cut into three-inch segments. Serve with
   ketchup for dipping.

Chapter 5: Pork & Lamb Favorites

Pork

Bacon-Wrapped Pork Tenderloin

Servings Provided: 4-6

Ingredients Needed:

- Pork tenderloin (1 lb.)
- Dijon mustard (1-2 tbsp.)
- Bacon (3-4 strips)

Preparation Technique:

1. Set the Air Fryer temperature at 360º Fahrenheit.
2. Coat the tenderloin with the mustard and wrap with the bacon.
3. Air-fry them for 15 minutes. Flip and cook 10 to 15 more minutes.
4. Serve with your favorite sides.

Crispy Breaded Pork Chops

Servings Provided: 6

Ingredients Needed:

- Center-cut boneless chops (6 @ .75-inch each)
- Kosher salt (.75 tsp.)
- Panko crumbs (.5 cup)
- Crushed cornflakes (.33 cup)
- Sweet paprika (1.25 tsp.)
- Large egg (1)
- Grated parmesan cheese (2 tbsp.)
- Onion (.5 tsp.)
- Garlic (.5 tsp.)
- Chili powder (.25 tsp.)
- Freshly cracked black pepper (.125 tsp.)

Preparation Technique:

1. Heat the Air Fryer to reach 400° Fahrenheit. Lightly spray the fry basket using a cooking spray.
2. Shake the salt over the chops.
3. Mix the cornflake crumbs, panko, salt, pepper, and chili powder.
4. Whisk the egg in another container. Dip the pork into the egg, then the crumb mixture, and add to the basket.
5. Prepare in two batches if needed. Cook for 12 minutes, flipping halfway through the frying cycle. Spritz both sides of the chops with cooking oil spray before browning.

Pork Meatballs

Servings Provided: 12

Ingredients Needed:

- Ground pork (12 oz.)
- Ground Italian sausage - mild or hot (8 oz.)
- Panko breadcrumbs (.5 cup)
- Egg (1)
- Salt (1 tsp.)
- Dried parsley (1 tsp.)
- Paprika (.5 tsp.)

Preparation Technique:

1. Set the Air Fryer at 350° Fahrenheit

2. Combine egg, sausage, pork, breadcrumbs, salt, parsley, and paprika in a large mixing container. Shape the mixture into 12 equally-sized meatballs and arrange on a baking tin.
3. Place half of the meatballs in the basket of the Air Fryer and cook for 8 minutes. Shake the basket and cook for two more minutes. Place onto the serving platter and wait for five minutes.
4. Repeat with remaining meatballs and use as desired.

Pork Taquitos

Servings Provided: 10

Ingredients Needed:

- Cooked shredded pork tenderloin or chicken (3 cups)
- Fat-free shredded mozzarella (2.5 cups)
- Flour tortillas (10 small)
- Lime juice (1 lime)

Preparation Technique:

1. Warm the Air Fryer to reach 380º Fahrenheit.
2. Sprinkle the juice over the pork and swirl it around.
3. To soften, microwave five tortillas at a time with a damp paper towel over them for 10 seconds.
4. Add three ounces of pork and 1/4 cup of cheese to each tortilla.
5. Tightly and gently roll the tortillas.
6. Line the tortillas onto a greased foil-lined pan.

7. Spray an even coat of cooking oil spray over the tortillas.
8. Air-fry for 7-10 minutes until tortillas are a golden color, flipping halfway through.
9. In case you don't have an Air Fryer, they can also be baked in the oven for 7 to 10 minutes on 375º Fahrenheit.

Ranch Pork Chops

Servings Provided: 4

Ingredients Needed:

- Center-cut - 1-inch boneless pork chops (4)
- Dry ranch salad dressing mix - ex. Hidden Valley (2 tsp.)
- Also Needed: Aluminum foil & cooking oil spray

Preparation Technique:

1. Warm the Air Fryer to 390º Fahrenheit.
2. Lightly spray both sides of the chops and the inside of the Air Fryer basket using a cooking oil spray. Sprinkle both sides with the ranch seasoning mix and let it rest at room temperature for ten minutes.
3. Place chops in the Air Fryer, working in batches if necessary, to ensure the fryer isn't overcrowded.
4. Cook for five minutes. Flip the chops and cook five minutes more. Let it rest on a foil-covered

plate for an additional five minutes before
serving.

Roast Pork Loin With Red Potatoes

Servings Provided: 2

Ingredients Needed:

- Large red potatoes (2)
- Pepper (1 tsp.)
- Salt (1 tsp.)
- Parsley (1 tsp.)
- Red pepper flakes (.5 tsp.)
- Garlic powder (.5 tsp.)
- Pork loin (2 lb.)
- A balsamic glaze from cooking

Preparation Technique:

1. Dice the potatoes.
2. Combine all of the seasonings and sprinkle over the potatoes and pork.
3. Arrange the pork and then the potatoes in the Air Fryer.
4. Secure the top and choose the roast button. Set the timer for 25 minutes at 400º Fahrenheit.
5. When done, wait for a few minutes before slicing.
6. Slice the pork loin into 4 to 5 sections. Add and serve the roasted potatoes in the serving dishes.
7. Use a balsamic glaze over the pork before serving.

Smoked Balsamic Raspberry Pork Chops

Servings Provided: 4

Ingredients Needed:

- Large eggs (2)
- Finely chopped pecans (1 cup)
- Japanese – panko breadcrumbs (1 cup)
- 2% milk (.25 cup)
- All-purpose flour (.25 cup)
- Smoked bone-in pork chops (4)
- Balsamic vinegar (.33 cup)
- Seedless raspberry jam (2 tbsp.)
- Brown sugar (2 tbsp.)
- Frozen orange juice concentrate - thawed (1 tbsp.)

Preparation Technique:

1. Set the Air Fryer at 400º Fahrenheit. Spritz the basket with cooking oil spray.
2. Whisk the milk and eggs in one dish and combine the pecans and breadcrumbs in another.
3. Prepare in batches. Dredge the pork chops through the flour - shaking off the excess. Dip them into the egg mix.
4. Prepare in single layers in the fryer 12-15 minutes, turning about halfway through the cooking cycle.
5. Combine the rest of the fixings in a saucepan, bringing it to a boil. Simmer 6 to 8 minutes until thickened. Serve over the chops.

Southern Fried Chops

Servings Provided: 5

Ingredients Needed:

- Pork chops (4)
- Buttermilk (3 tbsp.)
- All-purpose flour (.25 cup)
- Seasoning salt & black pepper (as desired)

Preparation Technique:

1. Set the fryer at 380º Fahrenheit.
2. Rinse and dry the chops using a paper towel. Season using the pepper and seasoning salt.
3. Drizzle the chops with the buttermilk and toss into a zipper-type bag with the flour. Marinate for 30 minutes.
4. Arrange the chops in the fryer (stacking is okay). Spritz using a cooking oil spray.
5. Air-fry the chops for 15 minutes (380º Fahrenheit). Flip after the first 10 minutes.
6. Serve with your favorite side dishes.

Lamb

Lamb Ribs - Saltimbocca

Servings Provided: 4

Ingredients Needed:

- Mozzarella cheese (2 balls)
- Lamb racks (2 lb.)
- Thinly sliced pieces of prosciutto (4)
- Sage leaves (4)
- Olive oil (2 tbsp.)

Preparation Technique:

1. Heat the Air Fryer to reach 350º Fahrenheit.
2. Slice the racks of lamb into quarters. Slice a deep pocket in each of the chops and stuff with thinly sliced cheese pieces.
3. Add a sage leaf on top and wrap with sliced prosciutto.
4. Spritz using one tablespoon of the oil. Set the timer for 15 minutes.
5. Transfer to a platter and serve.

Lamb & Turkey Meatballs

Servings Provided: 4

Ingredients Needed:

- Coriander (1 tbsp.)
- Mint (1 tbsp.)
- Ground lamb (1 lb.)
- Egg white (1)
- Turkey (4 oz.)
- Salt (.5 tsp.)
- Minced garlic cloves (2)
- Parsley (2 tbsp.)
- Olive oil (1 tbsp.)

Preparation Technique:

1. Heat the Air Fryer at 320º Fahrenheit.
2. Chop the mint and coriander.
3. Mix all of the fixings and shape into small meatballs.
4. Arrange in the Air Fryer and set the timer for 15 minutes.
5. Serve it with your favorite sauce.

Macadamia Crusted Roasted Rack Of Lamb

Servings Provided: 4-5

Ingredients Needed:

- Garlic (1 clove)
- Olive oil (1 tbsp.)
- Pepper and salt (to your liking)
- Rack of lamb (1.75 lb.)

Ingredients Needed - The Crust:

- Macadamia nuts (3 oz. unsalted)
- Fresh rosemary (1 tbsp.)
- Breadcrumbs (1 tbsp.)
- Egg (1)

Preparation Technique:

1. Set the Air Fryer at 220º Fahrenheit.
2. Dice the garlic clove into tiny bits. Make the garlic oil by mixing the pieces with the oil. Brush the lamb and season using salt and pepper.
3. Finely chop the nuts into a bowl and mix in the rosemary and breadcrumbs. Whisk the egg in another dish.
4. Dredge the lamb through the egg mixture and coat with the macadamia crust topping.
5. Arrange the rack of lamb in the Air Fryer basket—setting the timer for 30 minutes.
6. Lastly, raise the heat to 390º Fahrenheit and set the timer for an additional five minutes.

7. Take the lamb from the fryer and wait for about ten minutes. Cover with a tent of aluminum foil.
8. For Variation: Use cashews, pistachios, hazelnuts, or almonds.

Spicy Lamb Sirloin

Servings Provided: 4

Ingredients Needed:

- Boneless lamb sirloin steaks (1 lb.)
- Onion (half of 1)
- Salt (1 tsp.)
- Ginger (4 slices)
- Garlic (5 cloves)
- Ground fennel (1 tsp.)
- Ground cardamom (.5 tsp.)
- Garam masala (1 tsp.)
- Cayenne (.5 - 1 tsp.)
- Cinnamon (1 tsp.)

Preparation Technique:

1. Toss in all of the fixings into a blender, except the lamb chops.
2. Mix until the onion is finely minced, and everything is blended (3-4 min.).
3. Arrange the lamb chops into a large container. Use a sharp knife to slash the meat and fat. Add the blended spice paste. Combine thoroughly and pop it into the fridge for a minimum of 30 minutes or up to 24 hours.

4. Warm the Air Fryer. Set the fryer to 330º
   Fahrenheit for 15 minutes and add the lamb
   steaks in the fryer basket. Cook, flipping
   halfway through.
5. Use a meat thermometer to test the meat to
   make sure it's reached an internal temperature
   of 150º Fahrenheit for medium-well. Serve.

Chapter 6: Beef & Dinner Time Variety Options

Beef

Air Fried Beef & Potato

Servings Provided: 4

Ingredients Needed:

- Mashed potatoes (3 cups)

- Ground beef (1 lb.)
- Eggs (2)
- Garlic powder (2 tbsp.)
- Sour cream (1 cup)
- Freshly cracked black pepper (as desired)
- Salt (1 pinch)

Preparation Technique:

1. Set the Air Fryer to reach 390º Fahrenheit.
2. Combine all of the fixings in a mixing container. Scoop it into a heat-safe dish.
3. Arrange in the fryer to cook for two minutes.
4. Serve for lunch or a quick dinner.

Beef & Bacon Taco Rolls

Servings Provided: 2

Ingredients Needed:

- Ground beef (2 cups)
- Bacon bits (.5 cup)
- Tomato salsa (1 cup)
- Shredded Monterey Jack Cheese (1 cup)
- *As desired - with the beef taco spices:*
- Garlic powder
- Chili powder
- Black pepper
- Turmeric coconut wraps/your choice (4)

1. Warm the Air Fryer to reach 390º Fahrenheit.
2. Mix the beef and chosen spices, and add it to each of the fixings into the wraps.
3. Roll up the wraps and arrange them in the Air Fryer.
4. Set the timer for 15 minutes and serve.

Beef Empanadas

Servings Provided: 4

Ingredients Needed:

- Onion (1 small)
- Cloves of garlic (2)
- Olive oil (1 tbsp.)
- Ground beef (1 lb.)
- Empanada shells (1 pkg.)
- Green pepper (.5 of 1)
- Cumin (.5 tsp.)
- Tomato salsa (.25 cup)
- Egg yolk (1)
- Pepper and sea salt (to your liking)

Preparation Technique:

1. Peel and mince the garlic and onion. Deseed and dice the pepper.
2. Pour the oil to a skillet using the high-heat temperature setting.
3. Fry the ground beef until browned. Drain the grease and add the onions and garlic. Cook for 4

minutes. Combine the remainder of fixings (omitting the milk, egg, and shells for now). Cook using the low setting for 10 minutes.

4. Make an egg wash with the yolk and milk.
5. Add the meat to half of the rolled dough, brushing the edges with the wash. Fold it over and seal using a fork, brushing with the wash, and adding it to the basket.
6. Continue the process until all are done. Set the timer for 10 minutes in the Air Fryer at 350º Fahrenheit. Serve.

Beef Stew

Servings Provided: 6

Ingredients Needed:

- Butter (2 tsp.)
- Beef short ribs (10 oz.)
- Salt (.25 tsp.)
- Turmeric (1 tsp.)
- Chili flakes (.5 tsp.)
- Green pepper (1)
- Kale (4 oz.)
- Chicken stock (1 cup)
- Onion (half of 1)
- Green peas (4 oz.)

Preparation Technique:

1. Heat the Air Fryer at 360º Fahrenheit.

2. Measure the two teaspoons of butter to melt in the fryer basket. Add the ribs. Sprinkle with the salt, turmeric, and chili flakes. Set the timer to air-fry for 15 minutes.
3. Remove the seeds and chop the kale and green pepper. Dice the onion.
4. When the timer buzzes, pour in the stock, peppers, onions, peas, and the peeled garlic clove.
5. Stir well and add the chopped kale. Set the timer for eight more minutes before serving.

Black Peppercorns Meatloaf

Servings Provided: 4

Ingredients Needed:

- Parsley (1 tbsp.)
- Oregano (1 tbsp.)
- Basil (1 tbsp.)
- Salt and pepper (to your liking)
- Ground beef (4.5 lb.)
- Large onion (1 diced)
- Worcestershire sauce (1 tsp.)
- Tomato ketchup (3 tbsp.)
- Breadcrumbs (1 slice of bread if homemade)

Preparation Technique:

1. Set the temperature setting at 356º Fahrenheit.
2. Toss the beef, herbs, onion, Worcestershire sauce, and ketchup together and mix well (5

min.). Mix in the breadcrumbs.
3. Scoop the meatloaf into the baking dish and arrange it in the Air Fryer basket. Air-fry for 25 minutes.

Breaded Beef Schnitzel

Servings Provided: 1

Ingredients Needed:

- Olive oil (2 tbsp.)
- Thin beef schnitzel (1)
- Gluten-free breadcrumbs (.5 cup)
- Egg (1)

Preparation Technique:

1. Heat the Air Fryer a couple of minutes (356º Fahrenheit).
2. Combine the breadcrumbs and oil in a shallow bowl. Whisk the egg in another mixing container.
3. Dip the beef nto the egg, and then the breadcrumbs. Arrange in the basket of the Air Fryer.
4. Air-fry 12 minutes and serve.

Cheesy Beef Enchiladas

Servings Provided: 4

Ingredients Needed:

- Ground beef (1 lb.)
- Regular/Gluten-free taco seasoning (1 pkg.)
- Gluten-free tortillas (8)
- Black beans (1 can)
- Diced tomatoes (1 can)
- Mild chopped green chilies (1 can)
- Red enchilada sauce (1 can)
- Shredded Mexican Cheese (1 cup)
- Chopped fresh cilantro (1 cup)
- Sour cream (.5 cup)

Preparation Technique:

1. Set the Air Fryer temperature ahead of cooking time at 355º Fahrenheit. Line the fryer with a layer of foil if you choose.
2. Drain and rinse the beans. Drain the tomatoes and chiles.
3. Brown the ground beef in a skillet. Add in the taco seasoning.
4. Prepare four tortillas by adding beans, tomatoes, beef, and chilies.
5. Arrange the prepared tortillas in the basket of the Air Fryer.
6. After they are prepared, pour the enchilada sauce evenly over them, and garnish using the cheese.
7. Cook for five minutes in the Air Fryer.

8. Carefully remove, add the desired toppings, and
   serve.

Country Fried Steak

Servings Provided: 1

Ingredients Needed:

- Sirloin steak (1 - 6 oz.)
- Eggs (3)
- Panko (1 cup)
- Flour (1 cup)
- Pepper & salt (1 tsp. each)
- Garlic powder (1 tsp.)
- Onion powder (1 tsp.)
- Ground sausage (6 oz.)
- Pepper (1 tsp.)
- Flour (2 tbsp.)
- Milk (2 cups)

Preparation Technique:

1. Warm the Air Fryer to reach 370º Fahrenheit.
2. Use a meat mallet to beat the steak until thin. Add the seasonings with the panko.
3. Dredge the beef through the flour, egg, and panko.
4. Arrange the prepared steak in the basket. Set the timer for 12 minutes. Remove the steak.
5. Prepare the gravy. Cook the sausage and drain on a few paper towels, saving two tablespoons in the pan. Blend in the flour and sausage.
6. Pour in the milk and pepper, mixing until thickened.
7. Air-fry for three more minutes before serving.

Easy Rib Steak

Servings Provided: 2

Ingredients Needed:

- Steak rub - your preference (1 tbsp.)
- Rib steaks (2 lb.)
- Olive oil (1 tbsp.)

Preparation Technique:

1. Before it is time to cook, set the Air Fryer at 400º Fahrenheit.
2. Dust the steak using the oil and rub.
3. Place it in the basket to fry for 14 minutes, flipping after seven minutes.
4. Wait for at least 10 minutes before you slice to serve.

Inside Out Cheeseburgers

Servings Provided: 5

Ingredients Needed:

- Cheddar cheese (4 slices)
- Lean ground beef (.75 lb. or 12 oz.)
- Ketchup (4 tsp.)
- Minced onion (3 tbsp.)
- Salt & black pepper (as desired)
- Yellow mustard (2 tsp.)
- Dill pickle chips (8)

Preparation Technique:

1. Heat the Air Fryer at 370º Fahrenheit.
2. Dice the cheese into small pieces.
3. In a large mixing container, combine the ground beef, ketchup, pepper, salt, and mustard. Make four patties.
4. Place two burgers, side by side. Flatten the patty and add four pickle chips, and a layer of cheese.
5. Mash a patty on top, pressing the meat together tightly to enclose all of the fixings.
6. Arrange the burgers in the basket and cook for twenty minutes. Turn them over after about 10 minutes.
7. Serve the cheeseburgers on a bun with lettuce and tomatoes.

Mongolian Beef

Servings Provided: 4

Ingredients Needed:

- Flank steak (1 lb.)
- Cornstarch (.25 cup)
- *The Sauce:*
- Vegetable oil (2 tsp.)
- Ginger (.5 tsp.)
- Minced garlic (1 tbsp.)
- Soy sauce or Gluten-free soy sauce (.5 cup)
- Water (.5 cup)
- Brown sugar - packed (.75 cup)

- *Extras:*
- Cooked rice
- Green beans
- Green onions

Preparation Technique:

1. Set the temperature at 390º Fahrenheit.
2. Thinly slice the steak in long strips, then coat using the cornstarch.
3. Arrange in the Air Fryer and cook for 5 minutes per side.
4. While you're waiting for the steak cook, heat all of the sauce fixings in a medium-sized saucepan using the med-high heat setting.
5. Whisk each of the fixings together until it gets to a low-boil.
6. Once both the steak and sauce are cooked, place the steak in a bowl with the sauce and let it marinate in it for about 5 to 10 minutes.
7. When it's time to eat, use a set of tongs to remove the steak and let the excess sauce drip off.
8. Place the steak over the cooked rice and green beans, top with additional sauce if desired.

Roast Beef

Servings Provided: 6

Ingredients Needed:

- Garlic powder (.5 tsp.)
- Oregano (.5 tsp.)
- Dried thyme (1 tsp.)
- Olive oil (1 tbsp.)
- Round roast (2 lb.)

Preparation Technique:

1. Set the Air Fryer at 330º Fahrenheit.
2. Combine the spices. Brush the oil over the beef, and rub it using the spice mixture.
3. Add to a baking dish and arrange it in the Air Fryer basket for 30 minutes. Turn it over and continue cooking 25 more minutes.
4. Wait for a few minutes before slicing.
5. Serve on your choice of bread or plain with a delicious side dish.

Steak & Mushrooms

Servings Provided: 4

Ingredients Needed:

- Beef sirloin steak (1 lb.)
- Button mushrooms (8 oz./.25 cup)
- Worcestershire sauce (.25 cup)
- Olive oil (1 tbsp.)

- Parsley flakes (1 tsp.)
- Paprika (1 tsp.)
- Crushed chile flakes (1 tsp.)

Preparation Technique:

1. Slice the mushrooms. Cut the steak into one-inch cubes and combine with the mushrooms, Worcestershire sauce, olive oil, parsley, paprika, and chile flakes in a bowl.
2. Place a lid on the container and chill in the fridge for a minimum of four hours to overnight. About a half of an hour before you plan on preparing the steak, take it out of the fridge.
3. Warm the Air Fryer to 400° Fahrenheit.
4. Drain and discard the marinade from the steak mixture. Arrange the steak and mushrooms in the basket of the Air Fryer.
5. Set the timer for 5 minutes. Toss and cook for five more minutes.
6. Transfer the meal to a plate and wait for 5 minutes before serving.

Other Dinners

Bratwurst & Veggies

Servings Provided: 6

Ingredients Needed:

- Bratwurst (Approx 5 links/1 pkg.)
- Red & green bell pepper (1 each
- Onion - Red/Purple (.25 cup)
- Gluten-free cajun seasoning (.5 tbsp.)

Preparation Technique:

1. Warm the unit to reach 390° Fahrenheit.
2. Line the Air Fryer with foil, if preferred.
3. Slice and add in the vegetables.
4. Slice the bratwurst into about 0.5-inch size rounds, and place on top of the veggies.
5. Evenly sprinkle the seasoning on top.
6. Air-fry at for 10 minutes. Carefully open and stir or mix.
7. Finish air-frying for another 10 minutes.
8. Serve.

Stromboli

Servings Provided: 4

Ingredients Needed:

- Refrigerated pizza crust - homemade or store-bought (12 oz.)
- Sliced cooked ham (.33 lb.)
- Roasted red bell peppers (3 oz.)
- Mozzarella shredded cheese (.75 cup)
- Shredded cheddar cheese (3 cups)
- Milk (1 tbsp.)
- Egg yolk (1)

Preparation Technique:

1. Warm up the Air Fryer at 360º Fahrenheit.
2. Roll the dough to reach a ¼-inch thickness.
3. Add the peppers, ham, and cheese on one side of the dough and fold to close.
4. Whisk the milk and eggs to make an egg wash, and brush the dough.
5. Place the stromboli in the basket and set the timer for 15 minutes.
6. Check it at 5-minute intervals - flipping the stromboli for thorough cooking.

Chapter 7: Side Dishes & Appetizers

Air-Fried Okra

Servings Provided: 4

Ingredients Needed:

- All-purpose flour (.25 cup)
- Cornmeal (1 cup)
- Large egg (1)
- Okra pods (.5 lb)
- Salt (as desired)

Preparation Technique:

1. Set the Air Fryer to 400º Fahrenheit.
2. Whisk the egg in a shallow dish. Slice and stir in the okra.
3. Mix the cornmeal and flour in a gallon-size zipper plastic bag. Drop five slices of okra into the cornmeal mixture, zip the bag, and shake. Remove the breaded okra to a plate. Repeat with remaining okra slices.
4. Place half of the breaded slices into the fryer basket and mist using the cooking spray. Set the timer for four minutes. Shake the basket and mist okra with cooking oil spray again. Cook another four minutes. Shake the basket one last time and cook for another two minutes. Remove the okra from the basket and salt to your liking.
5. Repeat with the remaining okra slices.

Avocado & Bacon Fries

Servings Provided: 2

Ingredients Needed:

- Egg (1)
- Almond flour (1 cup)
- Bacon – cooked – small bits (4 strips)
- Avocados (2 large)
- *For Frying*: Olive oil

Preparation Technique:

1. Set the Air Fryer at 355º Fahrenheit.
2. Whisk the eggs in one container. Add the flour with the bacon in another.
3. Slice the avocado using lengthwise cuts. Dip into the eggs, then the flour mixture.
4. Drizzle oil in the fryer tray and cook for 10 minutes on each side or until they're the way you like them.

Battered Baby Ears Of Corn

Servings Provided: 4

Ingredients Needed:

- Carom seeds (.5 tsp.)
- Almond flour (1 cup)
- Chili powder (.25 tsp.)
- Garlic powder (1 tsp.)
- Boiled baby ears of corn (4)

- Baking soda (1 pinch)
- Salt (to your liking)

Preparation Technique:

1. Warm the Air Fryer to reach 350º Fahrenheit.
2. Whisk the flour, salt, garlic powder, baking soda, chili powder, and carom seeds.
3. Pour a little water into a bowl to make a batter. Dip the boiled corn in the mixture and arrange it in a foil-lined fryer basket.
4. Set the timer for 10 minutes.
5. Serve with your favorite entrée.

Breaded Avocado Fries

Servings Provided: 2

Ingredients Needed:

- Large avocado (1)
- Breadcrumbs (.5 cup)
- Egg (1)
- Salt (.5 tsp.)

Preparation Technique:

1. Warm the Air Fryer to reach 390º Fahrenheit.
2. Peel, remove the pit, and slice the avocado.
3. Prepare two shallow dishes, one with the breadcrumbs and salt, and one with a whisked egg.

4. Dip the avocado into the egg – then the breadcrumbs.
5. Add to the Air Fryer for ten minutes.
6. Serve as a side dish or an appetizer.

Brussels Sprouts

Servings Provided: 4-5

Ingredients Needed:

- Olive oil (5 tbsp.)
- Fresh brussels sprouts (1 lb.)
- Kosher salt (.5 tsp.)

Preparation Technique:

1. Prep the vegetables. Trim the stems and discard any damaged outer leaves. Cut into halves, rinse, and pat dry. Toss with the oil and salt.
2. Set the fryer temperature ahead of time to 390º Fahrenheit.
3. Toss the sprouts into the basket and air-fry for 15 minutes.
4. Shake the basket to ensure even browning.

Buffalo Cauliflower

Servings Provided: 4

Ingredients Needed:

- Breadcrumbs (1 cup)
- Cauliflower florets (4 cups)
- Buffalo sauce (.25 cup)
- Melted butter (.25 cup)
- *For the Dip*: Your preferred dressing

Preparation Technique:

1. Melt the butter in a microwaveable dish. Whisk in the buffalo sauce.
2. Dip the florets in the butter mixture. Use the stem as a handle, holding it over a cup and let the excess drip away.
3. Dredge the florets through the breadcrumbs. Drop them into the Air Fryer. Set the timer for 14 to 17 minutes at 350º Fahrenheit. (The unit *will not* need to preheat since it is calculated into the time.)
4. Shake the basket several times during the cooking process. Serve alongside your favorite dip, making sure to eat it right away because the crunchiness goes away quickly.
5. *Cooking Note:* Reheat in the oven. Don't use the microwave or it will be mushy.

Buttery Blossoming Onions

Servings Provided: 4

Ingredients Needed:

- Small onions (4)
- Dollops of butter (4)
- Olive oil (1 tbsp.)

Preparation Technique:

1. Preheat the Air Fryer to reach 350º Fahrenheit.
2. Peel the skin from the onion and remove the top and bottom to create flat ends.
3. Soak the onions in salted water for four (4) hours to remove its harshness.
4. Slice the onion as far down as you can without severing its body. Cut four times - making eight segments.
5. Toss the prepared onions into the fryer basket. Drizzle with oil, adding a dollop of butter to each one.
6. Cook in the fryer until the outside is dark (30 minutes).
7. *Note*: Four dollops equals about four (4) heaping tablespoons.

Charred Shishito Peppers

Servings Provided: 4

Ingredients Needed:

- Olive oil (1 tsp.)
- Juiced lemon (1)
- Shishito peppers (20)
- Sea salt (to taste)

Preparation Technique:

1. Set the Air Fryer at 390º Fahrenheit.
2. Toss the peppers in with the oil and salt. Add them to the basket and air-fry for five minutes.
3. Serve on a platter with a squeeze of lemon.

Crispy Onion Rings

Servings Provided: 2

Ingredients Needed:

- Coconut flour (2 tbsp.)
- Grated parmesan cheese (2 tbsp.)
- Egg (1)
- Large onion (1 in ringlets)
- Garlic powder (1 pinch)
- Pepper and salt (as desired)
- Olive oil (.25 cup)

Preparation Technique:

1. Whisk the flour, spices, and grated cheese.
2. Set the Air Fryer at 400º Fahrenheit.

3. Whisk the eggs in a separate mixing container and add the onion rings. Soak a minute or so, and dip into the flour mixture.
4. Place in the Air Fryer basket, setting the timer for 6 minutes per side.
5. Serve as a quick snack or favorite side dish.

Cumin Butternut Squash

Servings Provided: 4

Ingredients Needed:

- Butternut squash (1 medium)
- Cumin seeds (2 tsp.)
- Chili flakes (1 pinch)
- Salt & black pepper (as desired)
- Coriander (1 bunch)
- Pine nuts (.25 cup)
- Olive oil (1 tbsp.)
- Greek yogurt (.66 cup)

Preparation Technique:

1. Warm the Air Fryer temperature in advance to 380º Fahrenheit.
2. Cube the squash and toss using the spices and oil in a baking pan.
3. Add them to the Air Fryer for 20 minutes.
4. Toast the pine nuts. Serve with a portion of yogurt and garnish using a sprinkle of coriander.

Hasselback Potatoes

Servings Provided: 4

Ingredients Needed:

- Potatoes (4)
- Olive oil (as needed)

Preparation Technique:

1. Set the Air Fryer temperature at 356° Fahrenheit.
2. Peel the potatoes and slice in half, about 1/16-inches apart from the base. (You want to create a feathered effect by not cutting it all the way through.)
3. Gently brush the potatoes with oil. Position each one into the fryer for 15 minutes.
4. Brush again and air-fry for about 15 additional minutes until browned and well done.

Honey Roasted Carrots

Servings Provided: 4

Ingredients Needed:

- Carrots - baby or regular (3 cups)
- Honey (1 tbsp.)
- Olive oil (1 tbsp.)
- Pepper and salt (as desired)

Preparation Technique:

1. Heat the Air Fryer at 392° Fahrenheit. Dice the carrots into small chunks.
2. Combine the honey, oil, salt, pepper, and carrots in a mixing bowl, coating well.
3. Put the carrots into the Air Fryer and set the timer for 12 minutes.

Mediterranean Veggies

Servings Provided: 4

Ingredients Needed:

- Large cucumber (1)
- Green pepper (1)
- Large parsnip (1)
- Cherry tomatoes (.25 cup)
- Medium carrot (1)
- Garlic puree (2 tbsp.)
- Honey (2 tbsp.)
- Olive oil (6 tbsp.)
- Mixed herbs (1 tsp.)
- Pepper and salt (as desired)

Preparation Technique:

1. Warm the Air Fryer at 356° Fahrenheit.
2. Chop the cucumber and green pepper. Toss them into the Air Fryer.
3. Peel and dice the carrot and parsnip, adding the whole cherry tomatoes. Drizzle with three

tablespoons of oil. Set the timer for 15 minutes.

4. Mix the remainder of the fixings into an Air Fryer - safe baking dish.
5. Add the veggies to the marinade and shake well. Give it a sprinkle of pepper and salt and cook at 392º Fahrenheit for another five minutes.
6. *Note*: You can substitute different veggies, but don't use the cucumber and cauliflower in the same dish. Together, they produce too much liquid.
7. For variety, serve with a portion of honey and sweet potatoes to the mixture.

Mushroom Melt

Servings Provided:10

Ingredients Needed:

- Button mushrooms (10)
- Italian dried mixed herbs
- Salt and pepper
- Mozzarella cheese
- Cheddar cheese
- Optional Topping: Dried dill

Preparation Technique:

1. Rinse the mushrooms, remove the stems, and drain in a colander.
2. For the flavor, provide a pinch of chosen herbs, black pepper, salt, and olive oil.

3. Warm the Air Fryer to reach 356º Fahrenheit (3-5 min.).
4. Arrange the mushrooms in the basket with the hollow section facing you. Sprinkle the cheese on top of each of the caps.
5. Place the mushrooms in the cooker for 7 to 8 minutes.
6. Serve hot with a drizzle of basil or other tasty herbs.

Potato Hay

Servings Provided: 4

Ingredients Needed:

- Russet potatoes (2)
- Canola oil (1 tbsp.)
- Kosher salt and ground black pepper (as desired)

Preparation Technique:

1. Preheat the Air Fryer to 360º Fahrenheit.
2. Slice the potatoes into spirals using the medium grating attachment on a spiralizer, and with kitchen shears after 4 or 5 rotations.
3. Soak the spirals in a bowl of water for 20 minutes. Drain and rinse well. Pat potatoes dry with paper towels, removing as much moisture as possible.

4. Place the spirals in a large resealable plastic bag with the oil, salt, and pepper, tossing to coat.
5. Place half of the potato spirals in the fry basket and insert it into the Air Fryer. Set the timer for 5 minutes.
6. Increase temperature to 390º Fahrenheit. Pull out the fry basket and add the potato spirals using tongs. Return the bucket to the and continue cooking until golden brown for 10 to 12 minutes.
7. Reduce the temperature to 360º Fahrenheit and repeat with remaining potato spirals.

Semolina Veggie Cutlets

Servings Provided: 2

Ingredients Needed:

- Milk (5 cups)
- Veggies of choice - ex. carrots, cauliflower, peas, green beans, etc. (1.5 cups total)
- Olive oil – for frying
- Semolina (1 cup)
- Salt and pepper (as desired)

Preparation Technique:

1. Heat the milk in a saucepan (medium heat). When hot, add the vegetables, pepper, and salt. Set the timer for 3 minutes.
2. Mix in the semolina and air-fry for 10 minutes.
3. Prepare a baking sheet with a layer of parchment baking paper. Spread the mixture over the pan to chill in the fridge for a minimum of four hours.
4. Set the Air Fryer temperature to 350º Fahrenheit.
5. Remove the mixture from the fridge and slice into cutlets. Brush each one with oil and set the timer for 10 minutes.
6. Serve with a portion of hot sauce.

Smoked Cheese Asparagus

Servings Provided: 4

Ingredients Needed:

- Asparagus (1 lb.)
- Shredded smoked gouda cheese (.25 cup)
- Italian seasoning (2 tbsp.)
- Parmesan cheese (.5 cup)
- Sea salt (.5 tsp.)
- Freshly cracked black pepper (.25 tsp.)
- Heavy cream (1 cup)

Preparation Technique:

1. Set the Air Fryer temperature at 400º
   Fahrenheit.
2. Use a sharp knife to discard the ¼-inch portion
   each asparagus.
3. Whisk the heavy cream, Italian seasoning, and
   parmesan.
4. Arrange the asparagus in a shallow dish and
   cover with the mixture.
5. Place in the basket of the fryer. Set the timer for
   6 minutes.
6. Serve with the asparagus a sprinkle of cheese,
   pepper, and salt.

Sour Cream Stuffed Mushrooms

Servings Provided: 24 mushrooms

Ingredients Needed:

- Rashers of bacon/bacon with fat strips & meat
  (2 thinly sliced)
- Small carrot (1)
- Green pepper (half of 1)
- Grated cheese (1 cup)
- Sour cream (.5 cup)
- Mushrooms (24 medium-sized)

Preparation Technique:

1. Dice the onion, carrots, bacon, and mushroom
   stalks.
2. Slowly cook the veggies and bacon bits in a

saucepan until softened. Add the sour cream and cheese. Mix well.

3. Warm the Air Fryer for five minutes at 356º Fahrenheit. Air-fry for 8 minutes.

Sweet Potato Tots

Servings Provided: 4 / 6 each

Ingredients Needed:

- Peeled sweet potatoes (2 small/14 oz. total)
- Potato starch (1 tbsp.)
- Garlic powder (.125 tsp.)
- Kosher salt (1.25 tsp. - divided)
- No-salt-added ketchup (.75 cup)

Preparation Technique:

1. Set the Air Fryer to warm at 400° Fahrenheit.
2. Prepare a medium pot of water (high heat) and wait for it to boil. Add the potatoes and simmer until fork-tender (15 min.). Transfer them to a platter to cool (15 min.).
3. Grate the potatoes using the large holes of a box grater. Gently toss with garlic powder, potato starch, and one teaspoon of salt. Shape the mixture into about 24 (1-inch) tot-shaped cylinders.
4. Lightly coat the Air Fryer basket with a cooking oil spray. Place half of the tots (about 12) in a single layer in the fryer basket and spray with the cooking spray.

5. Cook until lightly browned, 12-14 minutes, turning the tots halfway through the cooking cycle. Remove from fryer basket and sprinkle with 1/8 teaspoon of salt. Repeat with the remaining tots.
6. Serve immediately with ketchup.

Thyme & Garlic Tomatoes

Servings Provided: 4

Ingredients Needed:

- Clove of garlic (1)
- Roma tomatoes (4)
- Dried thyme (.5 tsp.)
- Freshly ground black pepper & salt (as desired)
- Olive oil (1 tbsp.)

Preparation Technique:

1. Heat the Air Fryer at 390° Fahrenheit.
2. Mince the garlic clove. Slice the tomatoes and remove the pithy parts and seeds. Toss them into a mixing container along with the pepper, salt, thyme, garlic, and olive oil.
3. Arrange them in the Air Fryer with the cut side up. Set a timer for 15 minutes.
4. Cool for a few minutes. Add on top of poultry, fish, or pasta.

Chapter 8: Desserts Galore

Air Fried Plantains

Servings Provided: 4

Ingredients Needed:

- Avocado or sunflower oil (2 tsp.)
- Ripened/almost brown – plantains (2)
- *Optional:* Salt (.125 tsp.)

Preparation Technique:

1. Warm up the Air Fryer to 400º Fahrenheit.
2. Slice the plantains at an angle for a .5-inch thickness.
3. Mix the oil, salt, and plantains in a container – making sure you coat the surface thoroughly.
4. Set the timer for eight to ten minutes; shake after five minutes. If they are not done to your liking, add a minute or two more.

Air Fryer Beignets

Servings Provided: 7

Ingredients Needed:

- All-purpose flour (.5 cup)
- White sugar (.25 cup)
- Water (.125 cup)
- Large egg (1 separated)
- Melted butter (1.5 tsp.)
- Baking powder (.5 tsp.)
- Vanilla extract (.5 tsp.)

- Salt (1 pinch)
- Confectioners' sugar (2 tbsp.)
- Also Needed: Silicone egg-bite mold

Preparation Technique:

1. Warm the Air Fryer to reach 370º Fahrenheit. Spray the mold using a nonstick cooking spray.
2. Whisk the flour, sugar, water, egg yolk, butter, baking powder, vanilla extract, and salt together in a large mixing bowl. Stir to combine.
3. Using an electric hand mixer (medium speed), mix the egg white in a small bowl until soft peaks form. Fold into the batter. Pour the mixture into the mold using a small hinged ice cream scoop.
4. Arrange the filled silicone mold in the basket of the Air Fryer.
5. Cook for 10 minutes. Remove mold from the basket carefully, pop the beignets out, and flip them over onto a parchment paper-lined round.
6. Place the parchment round with beignets back into the fryer basket. Cook for another 4 minutes.
7. Remove the beignets from the Air Fryer basket and dust with confectioners' sugar.

Banana Smores

Servings Provided: 4

Ingredients Needed:

- Bananas (4)
- Mini-peanut butter chips (3 tbsp.)
- Graham cracker cereal (3 tbsp.)
- Mini-semi-sweet chocolate chips (3 tbsp.)

Preparation Technique:

1. Heat the Air Fryer in advance to 400° Fahrenheit.
2. Slice the un-peeled bananas lengthwise along the inside of the curve. *Don't slice through the bottom of the peel.* Open slightly - forming a pocket.
3. Fill each pocket with chocolate chips, peanut butter chips, and marshmallows. Poke the cereal into the filling.
4. Arrange the stuffed bananas in the fryer basket, keeping them upright with the filling facing up.
5. Air-fry until the peel has blackened, and the chocolate and marshmallows have toasted (6 minutes).
6. Cool for 1-2 minutes. Spoon out the filling to serve.

Blackberry & Apricot Crumble

Servings Provided: 6

Ingredients Needed:

- Fresh blackberries (5.5 oz.)
- Lemon juice (2 tbsp.)
- Fresh apricots (18 oz.)
- Sugar (.5 cup)
- Salt (1 pinch)
- Flour (1 cup)
- Cold butter (5 tbsp.)

Preparation Technique:

1. Heat the Air Fryer to 390º Fahrenheit.
2. Lightly grease an 8-inch oven dish with a spritz of cooking oil.
3. Remove the stones, cut the apricots into cubes, and put them in a container.
4. Combine the lemon juice, blackberries, and two tablespoons of sugar with the apricots and mix. Place the fruit in the oven dish.
5. Combine the salt, remainder of the sugar, and flour in a mixing container. Add one tablespoon of cold water and the butter, using your fingertips to make a crumbly mixture.
6. Crumble the mixture over the fruit, pressing them down.
7. Place the dish in the basket and slide it into the Air Fryer. Fry for 20 minutes. It is ready when it is cooked thoroughly, and the top is browned.

Blueberry Hand Pies

Servings Provided: 8

Ingredients Needed:

- Refrigerated pie crust (14 oz.)
- Blueberries (1 cup)
- Castor sugar (2.5 tbsp.)
- Lemon juice (1 tsp.)
- Salt (1 pinch)
- Water
- *Optional*: Vanilla sugar

Preparation Technique:

1. Heat the Air Fryer to reach 350° Fahrenheit.
2. Mix the sugar, lemon juice, salt, and blueberries in a medium mixing container.
3. Roll out the pie crusts and cut out six to eight 4-inch individual circles.
4. Scoop about one tablespoon of the blueberry filling in the center of each circle.
5. Moisten the edges of dough with a little water. Fold the dough over the filling to form a half-moon shape.
6. Using a fork, gently crimp the edges of the crust together. Then slice three slits on the top of the hand pies.
7. Spray the hand pies with a spritz of cooking oil spray. Sprinkle with vanilla sugar if using.
8. Place three to four hand pies in a single layer inside the Air Fryer basket.

9. Cook the pies for 9-12 minutes or until golden brown. Let each of the hand pies cool for at least 10 minutes before serving.

Brownies

Servings Provided: 2

Ingredients Needed:

- Granulated sugar (.5 cup)
- Cocoa powder (.33 cup)
- All-purpose flour (.25 cup)
- Baking powder (.25 tsp.)
- Pinch kosher salt
- Butter (.25 cup - melted and cooled slightly)
- Large egg (1)
- Also Needed: 6-inch round pan

Preparation Technique:

1. Prep the Air Fryer at 350° Fahrenheit.
2. Grease the pan with a cooking oil spray. In a medium mixing bowl, whisk to combine the sugar, cocoa powder, flour, baking powder, and salt.
3. In another mixing dish, whisk the melted butter and egg until combined. Add it all together and transfer the brownie batter to the prepared cake pan and smooth top.
4. Air-fry for 16-18 minutes, and let them cool ten minutes before slicing.

Caramel Cream-Dipped Apple Fries

Servings Provided: 8-10

Ingredients Needed:

- Honey-crisp apples/your choice (3)
- Graham cracker crumbs (1 cup)
- Eggs (3)
- Flour (.5 cup)
- Sugar (.25 cup)
- Whipped cream cheese (8 oz.)
- Caramel sauce (.5 cup + more for garnish)

Preparation Technique:

1. Peel and slice the apples into eight wedges. Toss the flour and apple slices together.
2. Prepare a dish with the eggs. Mix the sugar and crackers in another bowl. Dip the apples in the eggs, and then the crumb mixture coating all sides. Arrange on a baking tray.
3. Set the fryer to 380º Fahrenheit. Brush or spray the bottom of the Air Fryer with a spritz of oil.
4. Prepare in two batches using a single layer – spraying each batch lightly. Cook for 5 minutes and turn. Cook for another two minutes.
5. Make the cream dip by combining the caramel sauce and cream cheese.
6. Serve the hot apple fries with the caramel dip.

Cheesecake Egg Rolls

Servings Provided: 15 rolls

Ingredients Needed:

- Unchilled cream cheese (2 - 16 oz. pkg.)
- Granulated sugar (.5 cup)
- Lemon juice (1 tbsp.)
- Vanilla extract (1 tsp.)
- Fig jam (1- 8.5 oz. jar)
- Refrigerated ready-made egg roll wrappers (15)
- Egg wash: 1 tablespoon water + 1 egg beaten
- Olive oil cooking spray
- Unsalted butter (2 tbsp. - melted)
- Sugar (.25 cup)
- Ground cinnamon (1 tsp.)

Preparation Technique:

1. Use the mixing bowl of an electric mixer (with the whip attachment), combine the cream cheese, sugar, lemon juice, and vanilla extract. Mix well using medium speed for two minutes to combine. Remove the cheesecake filling and add it to a pastry bag or a zipper-top bag. Snip a corner.
2. Stir the jam, so it's easily scooped.
3. Prepare the egg roll wrapper with a pointed end toward you; in the center, pipe on approximately two tablespoons of cream cheese mixture. Add one tablespoon of jam. Use a pastry brush to coat the edges of the egg roll wrapper with egg wash. Fold the bottom corner over filling, roll snugly half-way to cover the

filling. Fold in both sides and roll the wrap, making sure it's corner is well-sealed. Spray the egg rolls with olive oil cooking spray on both sides.

4. Warm the Air Fryer to 370° Fahrenheit for ten minutes. Set aside to cool while the fryer heats.
5. Place four or five egg rolls in the hot fryer basket. Air-fry for five to seven minutes, or until the egg rolls are golden brown on top.
6. Remove the rolls from the basket and cool.
7. Lightly brush the rolls with melted butter. Combine sugar and cinnamon in a small bowl and sprinkle over egg rolls. Serve warm or at room temperature. Store any leftovers in the fridge.

Cherry Pie

Servings Provided: 8

Ingredients Needed:

- Cherry pie filling (21 oz. can)
- Milk (1 tbsp.)
- Refrigerated pie crusts (2)
- Egg yolk (1)

Preparation Technique:

1. Warm the fryer at 310° Fahrenheit.
2. Poke holes into the crust after placing it in a pie

plate. Allow the excess to hang over the edges.
Place in the Air Fryer for five (5) minutes

3. Transfer the basket with the pie plate onto the
   countertop. Fill it with the cherries. Remove the
   excess crust.
4. Cut the remaining crust into ¾-inch strips -
   placing weaving a lattice across the pie.
5. Make an egg wash with milk and egg. Brush the
   pie. Air-fry for 15 minutes. Serve with a scoop
   of ice cream.

Chocolate Cake

Servings Provided: 4

Ingredients Needed:

- Unchilled butter (1 stick)
- Cocoa powder (.33 cup)
- Baking powder (1 tsp.)
- Baking soda (.5 tsp.)
- Eggs (3)
- Sour cream (.5 cup)
- Flour (1 cup)
- Sugar (.66 cup)
- Vanilla (2 tsp.)

Preparation Technique:

1. Heat the Air Fryer to reach 320º Fahrenheit.
2. Mix the fixings using the low setting of an
   electric mixer.
3. Pour it into the basket and slide it into the Air
   Fryer.

4. Set the timer for 25 minutes. Once the timer
   buzzes, lightly push in the center to see if the
   cake is done. If it doesn't spring back when
   touched, air-fry for an additional 5 minutes.
5. Cool the cake and frost with your favorite icing.

Cinnamon Rolls

Servings Provided: 6

Ingredients Needed:

- Melted butter (2 tbsp. + more for brushing)
- Packed brown sugar (.33 cup)
- Ground cinnamon (.5 tsp.)
- Kosher salt
- All-purpose flour (as needed)
- Refrigerated Crescent rolls (8-oz. tube)
- *The Glaze*:
- Unchilled cream cheese (2 oz.)
- Powdered sugar (.5 cup)
- Whole milk (1 tbsp. + more if needed)

Preparation Technique:

1. Set the Air Fryer at 350° Fahrenheit.
2. Make the rolls. Prepare the Air Fryer with a
   sheet of parchment baking paper and brush with
   butter.

3. In a medium mixing container, combine the butter, brown sugar, cinnamon, and a large pinch of salt until smooth and fluffy.
4. Lightly flour a countertop, and roll the crescent rolls in one piece. Pinch seams together and fold in half. Roll into a 9x7-inch rectangle.
5. Spread the prepared butter mixture over the dough, leaving a 1/4-inch border. Starting at a long edge, roll up the dough like a jelly roll, then cut crosswise into six pieces.
6. Arrange the pieces in the fryer, cut-side upward - spaced evenly. Air-fry until golden and cooked through
7. Make the glaze. Whisk the powdered sugar, cream cheese, and milk together (adding milk by the teaspoonful, as needed for thinning the glaze.)
8. Finish it off by adding glaze over the rolls and serve.

Donut Bread Pudding

Servings Provided: 4

Ingredients Needed:

- Glazed donuts (6)
- Raw egg yolks (4)
- Whipping cream (1.5 cups)
- Sugar (.25 cups)
- Frozen sweet cherries (.75 cups)

- Cinnamon (1 tsp.)
- Semi-sweet chocolate baking chips (.5 cup)
- Raisins (.5 cup)

Preparation Technique:

1. Warm the Air Fryer at 310º Fahrenheit.
2. Toss the wet fixings in a container and add everything else.
3. Dump the mixture into a baking pan and cover it with foil. Place it into the basket and set the timer for one hour.
4. Chill the pudding thoroughly before serving.

Guilt-Free Paleo Pumpkin Muffins

Servings Provided: 12

Ingredients Needed:

- Pumpkin puree (1 cup)
- Gluten-free oats (2 cups)
- Honey (.0.5 cup)
- Medium eggs (2)
- Coconut butter (1 tsp.)
- Cocoa Nibs (1 tbsp.)
- Vanilla Essence (1 tbsp.)
- Nutmeg (1 tsp.)

Preparation Technique:

1. Warm the Air Fryer to reach Toss each of the fixings into the blender and mix until smooth.

2. Place the muffin mix into little muffin cases,
   spreading it out over 12 separate ones.
3. Arrange it in the Air Fryer and set the timer for
   15 minutes on 356⁰ Fahrenheit.
4. Serve when cool.

Iced Strawberry Cupcakes

Servings Provided: 10

Ingredients Needed:

- Butter (.5 cup +.5 cup)
- Caster sugar (.5 cup)
- Medium eggs (2)
- Vanilla essence (.5 tsp.)
- Self-rising flour (.5 cup)
- Icing sugar (.5 cup)
- Whipped cream (1 tbsp.)
- Pink food coloring (.5 tsp.)
- Fresh (blended) strawberries (.25 cup)

Preparation Technique:

1. Heat the Air Fryer to reach 338⁰ Fahrenheit.
2. Combine the butter and sugar in a large mixing
   bowl until it's creamy smooth. Break the eggs
   into the mix one at a time, along with the vanilla
   essence.
3. Blend in a small amount of flour at a time until
   all is thoroughly mixed.

4. Dump the mixture into greased ramekins, about 75% of the way full. Arrange them in the Air Fryer for eight minutes.
5. *Make the Frosting:* Cream the butter and slowly mix in the icing sugar until creamy. Pour in the food coloring, (blended) strawberries, and whipped cream—mix well.
6. Take them out and use a piping bag to make the swirl frosting for a tasty, fancy cupcake - every time.

Molten Lava Cakes

Servings Provided: 4

Ingredients Needed:

- Self-rising flour (1.5 tbsp.)
- Baker's Sugar - not powdered (3.5 tbsp.)
- Unsalted Butter (3.5 oz.)
- Dark Chocolate (Pieces or Chopped- (3.5 oz.)
- Eggs (2)
- Also Needed: 4 Standard-sized oven-safe ramekins & microwave safe bowl

Preparation Technique:

1. Warm the Air Fryer to 375° Fahrenheit.
2. Grease and flour the ramekins.
3. Melt the chocolate and butter in the microwave on level 7 (3 min.) stirring thoroughly.
4. Whisk the eggs and sugar until pale and frothy.

5. Mix the melted chocolate mixture into the egg
    mixture. Stir in flour. Use a spatula to combine
    everything.
6. Fill the ramekins about ¾ of the way to full with
    the cake. Set the timer for 10 minutes.
7. Remove from the Air Fryer and cool in ramekins
    for two minutes.
8. Carefully turn the ramekins upside down onto a
    serving plate, tapping the bottom with a butter
    knife to loosen edges. The cake should release
    from ramekin with little effort, and the center
    should appear dark/gooey.
9. Enjoy warm with a raspberry drizzle.

Smores

Servings Provided: 4

Ingredients Needed:

- Whole graham crackers (4)
- Marshmallows (2)
- Chocolate - such as Hershey's (4 pieces)

Preparation Technique:

1. Break the graham crackers in half to make eight
    squares. Cut marshmallows in half crosswise
    with a pair of scissors.
2. Place the marshmallows cut side down on four
    graham squares. Place marshmallow side up in
    the basket of the Air Fryer and cook on 390°

Fahrenheit for four to five minutes, or until
golden.

3. Remove them from the fryer and place a piece
Break all graham crackers in half to create eight
squares. Cut marshmallows in half crosswise
with a pair of scissors.

4. Place marshmallows cut side down on four
graham squares. of chocolate and graham
square on top of each toasted marshmallow and
serve.

Yam & Marshmallow Hand Pies

Servings Provided: 4

Ingredients Needed:

- Candied yams (16 oz. can)
- Crescent dough sheet/homemade crust (1)
- Cinnamon (.5 tsp.)
- Allspice (.25 tsp.)
- Salt (.25 tsp.)
- Marshmallow crème (2 tbsp.)
- Egg (1)
- The Maple Glaze:
- Confectioners' sugar (.5 cup)
- Maple syrup (.5 cup)

Preparation Technique:

1. Warm the Air Fryer at 400º Fahrenheit.
2. Drain the syrup from the yams and combine
   with the cinnamon, salt, and allspice using a

fork until thoroughy mixed.

3. Put the dough sheet onto a board and cut it into four equal segments.
4. Spoon the filling onto the squares and add a tablespoon of the crème.
5. Use a brush to spread the egg over the edges of the dough and place the remainder of the two pieces of dough on top of the pies.
6. Use a fork to crimp the edges and cut three slits in the top for venting.
7. Arrange in the Air Fryer for six minutes.
8. Prepare the glaze using the sugar and syrup in a small dish—slowly adding the syrup—until the sugar dissolves.
9. To serve, drizzle the glaze over the warm pies and enjoy.

Chapter 9: Delicious Ketogenic Air Fried Specialties

I hope you're ready to begin your ketogenic journey using your Air Fryer. You will learn many different ways you can stay in tune with your keto diet plan. The keto diet plan goes by many different names such as the low-carb diet and the low-carbohydrate diet & high-fat (LCHF) diet plan.

If you are not on the keto plan, consider this; your liver produces ketones which are used as energy to provide adequate levels of proteins similar to other low carbohydrate diet techniques. The process known as ketosis is natural and happens every day.

The recipes contained in this segment are made explicitly for you since they are calculated with the macros to keep your diet plan running smoothly. (They are also delicious, even if you aren't trying to manage ketosis!)

Breakfast

Air Bread & Egg Butter:

For the Bread

Servings Provided: 19

Nutritional Facts Per Serving:

- **Protein Count**: 1.2 grams
- **Net Carbohydrates**: 0.5 grams
- **Total Fat Content**: 3.9 grams
- **Calorie Count**: 40

Ingredients Needed:

- Eggs (3)
- Baking powder (1 tsp.)
- Sea salt (.25 tsp.)
- Almond flour (1 cup)
- Unchilled butter (.25 cup)

Preparation Technique:

1. Set the Air Fryer at 350º Fahrenheit.
2. Whisk the eggs with a hand mixer. Mix in the rest of the fixings to make a dough. Knead the dough and cover using a tea towel for about ten minutes.
3. Air-fry the bread 15 minutes. Remove the bread and let it cool down on a wooden board.
4. Slice and serve with your favorite meal or as it is with butter (below).

For the Butter:

Servings Provided: 4

Nutritional Facts Per Serving:

- **Protein Count**: 3 grams
- **Net Carbohydrates**: 2.67 grams
- **Total Fat Content**: 8.5 grams
- **Calorie Count**: 164

Ingredients Needed:

- Eggs (4)
- Salt (1 tsp.)
- Butter (4 tbsp.)

Preparation Technique:

1. Prepare the Air Fryer basket using a layer of foil and add the eggs.
2. Air-fry the eggs at 320º Fahrenheit for 17 minutes. Transfer to an ice-cold water bath to chill.
3. Peel and chop the eggs and combine with the rest of the fixings. Enjoy with your *Air Fried Bread*.

Asparagus Omelet

Servings Provided: 2

Nutritional Facts Per Serving:

- **Protein Count**: 15 grams
- **Net Carbohydrates**: 2 grams
- **Total Fat Content**: 23 grams
- **Calorie Count**: 287

Ingredients Needed:

- Eggs (3)
- Pepper & salt (1 pinch each)
- Steamed asparagus tips (5)
- Warm water (2 tbsp.)
- Parmesan cheese (1 tbsp.)

Preparation Technique:

1. Set the Air Fryer temperature setting to 320º Fahrenheit.
2. Whisk the eggs, water, pepper, salt, and cheese.
3. Spritz a skillet with cooking oil spray and steam the asparagus. Add to the fryer basket. Pour in the egg mixture.
4. Fry for 5 minutes and serve.

Bacon Egg & Cheese Roll-Ups

Servings Provided: 4

Nutritional Facts Per Serving:

- **Protein Count**: 28.2 grams
- **Net Carbohydrates**: 5.3 grams
- **Total Fat Content**: 31.7 grams
- **Calorie Count**: 460

Ingredients Needed:

- Unsalted butter (2 tbsp.)
- Chopped onion (.25 cup)
- Almond flour (1 cup)
- Medium green bell pepper (half of 1)
- Large eggs (6)
- Shredded sharp cheddar cheese (1 cup)
- Sugar-free bacon (12 slices)
- For Dipping: Mild salsa (.5 cup)

Preparation Technique:

1. Prepare a skillet using the medium heat temperature setting to melt butter.
2. Discard the seeds and dice the peppers and onion. Toss them into the pan and sauté for three minutes.
3. Whisk the eggs in another small mixing bowl, and pour into the pan. Scramble the eggs with the onions and peppers about five minutes or until fluffy and fully cooked. Take it away from the heat and set aside.
4. Heat the Air Fryer to reach 350º Fahrenheit.
5. Arrange three slices of bacon side by side. You can overlap them about 1/4-inch. Divide the eggs in a pile (on the side that's the closest to you). Garnish the top of the eggs with a portion of cheese.
6. Roll the bacon tightly around the eggs. Hold them together using a toothpick or skewer if necessary. Arrange each of the rolls into the Air Fryer basket.
7. Air-fry them for 15 minutes. Turn the rolls halfway through the cooking time.
8. The bacon will be browned and crispy when done.
9. Serve immediately with salsa for dipping. It's great for brunch!

Brunch Ham Hash

Servings Provided: 3

Nutritional Facts Per Serving:

- **Protein Count**:33.2 grams
- **Net Carbohydrates**: 5.9 grams
- **Total Fat Content**: 23.7 grams
- **Calorie Count**: 372

Ingredients Needed:

- Parmesan cheese (5 oz.)
- Ham (10 oz.)
- Onion (half of 1)
- Butter (1 tbsp.)
- Egg (1)
- Paprika (1 tsp.)
- Freshly ground black pepper (1 tsp.)
- Also Needed: 3 ramekins

Preparation Technique:

1. Set the Air Fryer at 350º Fahrenheit.
2. Peel and dice the onion. Slice the ham into small strips and shred the parmesan cheese.
3. Lastly, whisk the egg, salt, pepper, and paprika; and add to the remainder of the fixings.
4. Sprinkle with pepper, paprika, and salt. Pour into the ramekins and sprinkle with the parmesan. Arrange the ramekins in the Air Fryer for 10 minutes.
5. When ready, remove from the fryer, and scramble.

Dark Chocolate Avocado Muffins

Servings Provided: 7

Nutritional Facts Per Serving:

- **Protein Count**: 2.2 grams
- **Net Carbohydrates**: 2.9 grams
- **Total Fat Content**: 12.4 grams
- **Calorie Count**: 133

Ingredients Needed:

- Almond flour (1 cup)
- Baking soda (.5 tsp.)
- Apple cider vinegar (1 tsp.)
- Egg (1)
- Butter (4 tbsp.)
- Stevia powder (3 scoops)
- Pitted avocado (.5 cup)
- Melted dark chocolate (1 oz.)

Preparation Technique:

1. Set the Air Fryer temperature at 355º Fahrenheit.
2. Whisk the almond flour, baking soda, vinegar, stevia powder, and melted chocolate.
3. Whisk the egg in another container and add to the mixture along with the butter.
4. Peel, cube, and mash the avocado and add. Mix using a hand mixer to make the flour mixture smooth. Pour into muffin forms (½ full).
5. Set the timer for 9 minutes.
6. Lower the heat (340º Fahrenheit) and air-fry three additional minutes.

7. Chill before serving for the best results.

Eggs - Ham & Spinach

Servings Provided: 4

Nutritional Facts Per Serving:

- **Protein Count**: 15 grams
- **Net Carbohydrates**: 3 grams
- **Total Fat Content**: 13 grams
- **Calorie Count**: 190

Ingredients Needed:

- Sliced ham (7 oz.)
- Spinach (2.25 cups)
- Cream milk (4 tsp.)
- Olive oil (1 tbsp.)
- Large eggs (4)
- Salt and pepper (to your liking)
- Also Needed:
- Ramekins (4)
- 1 Skillet

Preparation Technique:

1. Set the Air Fryer temperature to 356º Fahrenheit. Spray the ramekins.
2. Warm up the oil in a skillet (med. heat) and saute the spinach until wilted. Drain.
3. Divide the spinach and rest of the fixings in each of the ramekins.

4. Sprinkle with salt and pepper. Bake until set (20 min.).
5. Serve when they are to your liking.

Pumpkin Pie French Toast

Servings Provided: 4

Nutritional Facts Per Serving:

- **Protein Count**: 8 grams
- **Net Carbohydrates**: 3 grams
- **Total Fat Content**: 19 grams
- **Calorie Count**: 267

Ingredients Needed:

- Water (.25 cup)
- Large eggs (2)
- Pumpkin puree (.25 cup)
- Pumpkin pie spices (.25 tsp.)
- Butter (.25 cup)
- Low-carb bread (4 slices)

Preparation Technique:

1. Warm up the fryer to reach 340ºFahrenheit before fry time.
2. Whisk the eggs, water, pie spice, and pumpkin puree.
3. Once it's smooth, dip the bread into the mixture.
4. Arrange each slice in the fryer and set the timer for 10 minutes.
5. Serve with a portion of butter.

Scrambled Pancake Hash

Servings Provided: 7

Nutritional Facts Per Serving:

- **Protein Count**: 4.4 grams
- **Net Carbohydrates**: 10.7 grams
- **Total Fat Content**: 13.3 grams
- **Calorie Count**: 178

Ingredients Needed:

- Coconut flour (1 cup)
- Ground ginger (1 tsp.)
- Salt (1 tsp.)
- Baking soda (1 tsp.)
- Apple cider vinegar (1 tbsp.)
- Heavy cream (.25 cup)
- Egg (1)
- Butter (5 tbsp.)

Preparation Technique:

1. Heat the Air Fryer to 400º Fahrenheit.
2. Whisk the baking soda, flour, ginger, and salt in a mixing container.
3. In another mixing container, add the egg, butter, and cream. Blend well using a hand mixer.
4. Combine the fixings and mix until smooth.
5. Carefully pour the mixture into the fryer basket tray and cook for four (4) minutes.
6. Remove and scramble the hash. Air-fry for another five minutes.
7. Transfer to a serving platter.

Thai Omelet

Servings Provided: 4

Nutritional Facts Per Serving:

- **Protein Count**: 11 grams
- **Net Carbohydrates**: 2.2 grams
- **Total Fat Content**: 11 grams
- **Calorie Count**: 253

Ingredients Needed:

- Fish sauce (2 tbsp.)
- Eggs (4)
- White pepper powder (2 tbsp.)
- Shallot (1)
- Garlic (2 cloves)
- Lime juice (half of 1 lime)
- Sausage (.5 cup)
- Green onion (1)
- Fresh spinach (1 handful)
- For the Pan: Olive oil or keto-friendly option (as needed)
- For the Garnish: Cilantro

Preparation Technique:

1. Warm the fryer to reach 340º Fahrenheit.
2. Mince the shallots, garlic, and green onions. Finely chop the sausage.
3. Heat the oil in a skillet. Whisk the eggs in a large mixing container. Mix in with the pepper and fish sauce.

4. Whisk well and add the remainder of the fixings until combined.
5. Pour into the pan and place it into the Air Fryer Basket.
6. Air-fry for 10 minutes.
7. Garnish with the cilantro and serve.

Tofu Egg Muffins

Servings Provided: 4

Nutritional Facts Per Serving:

- **Protein Count**: 9 grams
- **Net Carbohydrates**: 1 gram
- **Total Fat Content**: 5 grams
- **Calorie Count**: 97

Ingredients Needed:

- Small tofu chunk (1 cut in cubes)
- Large eggs (3)
- Sesame oil (.25 tsp.)
- Ground cumin (.25 tsp.)
- Ground coriander (.25 tsp.)
- Black pepper (.25 tsp.)
- Soy sauce substitute - ex: Keto-friendly is liquid aminos (.5 tsp.)
- Spring onion (1 handful)
- Coriander (1 handful)
- Also Needed: 4 muffin molds

Preparation Technique:

1. Set the Air Fryer at 392º Fahrenheit (5 min.).
2. Chop the coriander and onion. Combine all of the fixings (omit the tofu for now). Whisk well.
3. Break the tofu into equal portions in the mold. Pour the mixture over each one.
4. Place in the Air Fryer for 10 minutes and serve.

Turkey "Sausage" Patties

Servings Provided: 6

Nutritional Facts Per Serving:

- **Protein Count**: 16.3 grams
- **Net Carbohydrates**: 10.2 grams
- **Total Fat Content**: 12.2 grams
- **Calorie Count**: 302

Ingredients Needed:

- Large garlic clove (1)
- Small onion (1)
- Olive oil (1 tsp.)
- Pepper and salt (to your liking)
- Chopped chives (1 tbsp.)
- Paprika (.75 tsp.)
- Nutmeg (1 pinch)
- Fennel seeds (1 tsp.)
- Vinegar (1 tbsp.)
- Lean ground turkey (1 lb.)

Preparation Technique:

1. Heat the Air Fryer to reach 375º Fahrenheit.
2. Mince the onion and garlic.
3. Pour half of the oil with the garlic and onion into the Air Fryer. Cook for 1 minute; add the seeds and place them on a platter.
4. Combine the paprika, nutmeg, pepper, salt, chives, onion, turkey, and vinegar. Mix well and shape into patties.
5. Add the remainder of the oil and air fry the patties for three minutes.
6. Serve the substitute "sausage" patties on keto-friendly buns.

Lunch:

Bacon-Wrapped Chicken

Servings Provided: 3

Nutritional Facts Per Serving:

- **Protein Count**: 30.5 grams
- **Net Carbohydrates**: 0.6 grams
- **Total Fat Content**: 26 grams
- **Calorie Count**: 364

Ingredients Needed:

- Breast of chicken (1)
- Unsmoked bacon (6 strips)
- Soft garlic cheese (1 tbsp.)

Preparation Technique:

1. Slice the chicken into six pieces.
2. Spread the garlic cheese over each bacon strip. Add a piece of chicken to each one. Roll and secure with a toothpick.
3. Prepare the Air Fryer and let it warm up for about 3 minutes. Arrange the wraps in the fryer basket. Air-fry for about 15 minutes.

Beef Roll-Ups

Servings Provided: 4

Nutritional Facts Per Serving:

- **Protein Count**: 16.3 grams
- **Net Carbohydrates**: 9.8 grams
- **Total Fat Content**: 12.3 grams
- **Calorie Count**: 282

Ingredients Needed:

- Pesto (3 tbsp.)
- Beef flank steak (2 lb.)
- Fresh baby spinach (.75 cup)
- Roasted red bell peppers (3 oz.)
- Provolone cheese (6 slices)
- Sea salt and black pepper (as desired)

Preparation Technique:

1. Set the Air Fryer in advance to 400º Fahrenheit.
2. Slice the steak open, but not all the way through. Spread the pesto over the steak.
3. Layer and add the peppers, cheese, and spinach (¾ of the way into the meat). Dust it using a sprinkle of pepper and salt.
4. Roll the wraps and securely close each one using toothpicks to hold it together.
5. Set the timer for 14 minutes – turning the roll-ups about halfway through the frying cycle.
6. When the cycle is completed, wait for about 10 minutes before slicing to serve.

Chicken Hash

Servings Provided: 3

Nutritional Facts Per Serving:

- **Protein Count**: 21 grams
- **Net Carbohydrates**: 7.1 grams
- **Total Fat Content**: 16.8 grams
- **Calorie Count**: 261

Ingredients Needed:

- Salt (1 pinch)
- Back pepper (1 tsp.)
- Chicken fillet (7 oz.)
- Cauliflower (6 oz. or 1 medium)
- Yellow onion (half of 1)
- Green pepper (1)
- Water (1 tbsp.)
- Butter (3 tbsp.)
- Cream (1 tbsp.)

Preparation Technique:

1. Warm the Air Fryer to reach 380º Fahrenheit.
2. Dice the onion. Chop the green peppers and cauliflower. Toss into a blender to make rice. Chop the chicken into chunks. Sprinkle using pepper and salt.
3. Prepare the veggies and combine the fixings.
4. Add them to the fryer basket and cook until done (6-7 min.).
5. Serve anytime for lunch or a snack.

Dragon Shrimp

Servings Provided: 2

Nutritional Facts Per Serving:

- **Protein Count**: 31 grams
- **Net Carbohydrates**: 5.2 grams
- **Total Fat Content**: 27 grams
- **Calorie Count**: 405

Ingredients Needed:

- Almond flour (.25 cup)
- Ginger (1 pinch)
- Chopped onions (1 cup)
- Shrimp (.5 lb.)
- Eggs (2)
- Soya sauce (.5 cup)
- Olive oil (2 tbsp.)

Preparation Technique:

1. Heat the Air Fryer to reach 390º Fahrenheit.
2. Boil the shrimp for about five minutes.
3. Make a paste from the mixture of mashed onions and ginger.
4. Whisk the eggs and add with the rest of the fixings.
5. Add the shrimp to the mixture and air-fry for 10 minutes.
6. Serve with a dish of keto-friendly mayo.

Fish Nuggets

Servings Provided: 4

Nutritional Facts Per Serving:

- **Protein Count**: 25 grams
- **Net Carbohydrates**: 10 grams
- **Total Fat Content**: 20 grams
- **Calorie Count**: 334

Ingredients Needed:

- Cod fillet (1 lb.)
- Eggs (3)
- Olive oil (4 tbsp.)
- Almond flour (1 cup)
- Gluten-free breadcrumbs (1 cup)
- Salt (1 tsp.)

Preparation Technique:

1. Preset the temperature of the Air Fryer at 390° Fahrenheit.
2. Slice the cod into nuggets.
3. Prepare three bowls. Beat the eggs in one. Combine the salt, oil, and breadcrumbs in another. Sift the almond flour into the third one.
4. Cover each of the nuggets with the flour, dip in the eggs, and the breadcrumbs.
5. Arrange the breaded nuggets into the basket and set the timer for 20 minutes.

Roast Beef For Sandwiches

Servings Provided: 6

Nutritional Facts Per Serving:

- **Protein Count**: 16.8 grams
- **Net Carbohydrates**: 11.7 grams
- **Total Fat Content**: 12.8 grams
- **Calorie Count**: 304

Ingredients Needed:

- Oregano (.5 tsp.)
- Garlic powder (.5 tsp.)
- Dried thyme (1 tsp.)
- Olive oil (1 tbsp.)
- Round roast (2 lb.)

Preparation Technique:

1. Warm the Air Fryer to reach 330º Fahrenheit.
2. Combine the spices. Brush the oil over the beef and rub in the spice mixture.
3. Arrange the roast in a baking dish. Place it in the fryer for 30 minutes. Flip it over and continue frying another 25 minutes.
4. Wait for a few minutes before slicing.
5. Serve on your choice of keto-friendly bread for a delicious sandwich or serve with a favorite side dish.

Turkey & Avocado Burrito

Servings Provided: 2

Nutritional Facts Per Serving:

- **Protein Count**: 12.3 grams
- **Net Carbohydrates**: 9.7 grams
- **Total Fat Content**: 11.2 grams
- **Calorie Count**: 289

Ingredients Needed:

- Eggs (4)
- Pepper & Salt (as desired)
- Salsa (4 tbsp.)
- Sliced avocado (.5 cup)
- Cooked turkey breast (8 slices)
- Grated mozzarella cheese (.25 cup)
- Sliced red bell pepper (half of 1)
- Tortillas (2)

Preparation Technique:

1. Preheat the Air Fryer at 390º Fahrenheit for 5 minutes, and spray the fryer tray with a spritz of cooking oil spray.
2. Whisk the eggs, pepper, and salt. Add the eggs to a skillet. When done, add the eggs to the tortillas.

3. Prepare the burrito beginning with a layer of
   turkey, avocado, peppers, cheese, and salsa.
   Roll it up slowly.
4. Spray the fryer and arrange the burritos in the
   basket. Prepare for 5 minutes.
5. Serve warm.

Dinner

Chicken Strips

Servings Provided: 4

Nutritional Facts Per Serving:

- **Protein Count**: 33 grams
- **Net Carbohydrates**: 0.6 grams
- **Total Fat Content**: 11.5 grams
- **Calorie Count**: 245

Ingredients Needed:

- Paprika (1 tsp.)
- Chicken fillets (1 lb.)
- Cream (1 tbsp.)
- Pepper and salt (.5 tsp.)

Preparation Technique:

1. Slice the chicken into fillet strips. Sprinkle using pepper and salt.
2. Set the Air Fryer at 365º Fahrenheit.
3. Arrange the strips in the basket and air-fry for 6 minutes.
4. Flip the strips and cook another 5 minutes.
5. Garnish using the cream and paprika. Serve warm.

Creamy Salmon

Servings Provided: 2

Nutritional Facts Per Serving:

- **Protein Count**: 41 grams
- **Net Carbohydrates**:13 grams
- **Total Fat Content**: 25 grams
- **Calorie Count**: 426

Ingredients Needed:

- Chopped dill (1 tbsp.)
- Salt (1 pinch)
- Olive oil (1 tbsp.)
- Sour cream (3 tbsp.)
- Plain yogurt (1.76 oz.)
- Salmon (.75 lb./6 pieces)

Preparation Technique:

1. Heat the Air Fryer and wait for it to reach 285º Fahrenheit.
2. Shake the salt over the salmon and add them to the fryer basket with the olive oil to air-fry for 10 minutes.
3. Whisk the yogurt, salt, and dill.
4. Serve the salmon with the sauce with your favorite sides.

Shrimp Scampi

Servings Provided: 4

Nutritional Facts Per Serving:

- **Protein Count**: 23 grams
- **Net Carbohydrates**: 1 gram
- **Total Fat Content**: 13 grams
- **Calorie Count**: 221

Ingredients Needed:

- Lemon juice (1 tbsp.)
- Butter (4 tbsp.)
- Minced garlic (1 tbsp.)
- Dried chives (1 tsp.) or Chopped chives (1 tbsp.)
- Red pepper flakes (2 tsp.)
- Dried (1 tsp.) or Minced basil leaves (1 tbsp.) plus more for sprinkling
- Chicken stock or white wine (2 tbsp.)
- Defrosted shrimp (1 lb. or about 21-25 count)
- Also Needed: 6x3 metal pan and silicone mitts

Preparation Technique:

1. Heat the Air Fryer at 330º Fahrenheit. Also, warm the skillet.
2. Add the pepper flakes, garlic, and butter into the hot pan and sauté for about 2 minutes. Stir once to infuse the garlic.
3. Open the Air Fryer and add the shrimp. Air-fry for 5 minutes, stirring once.

4. Remove the pan using oven mitts. The shrimp
   will continue cooking, but let it sit on the
   countertop to cool.
5. Stir well and dust with a layer of freshly chopped
   basil leaves to serve.

Stuffed Pork Chops

Servings Provided: 3

Nutritional Facts Per Serving:

- **Protein Count**: 28 grams
- **Net Carbohydrates**: 1.2 grams
- **Total Fat Content**: 28 grams
- **Calorie Count**: 412

Ingredients Needed:

- Salt and pepper (as desired)
- Thick-cut pork chops (3)
- Mushrooms (7)
- Lemon juice (1 tbsp.)
- Almond flour (1 tbsp.)

Preparation Technique:

1. Heat the Air Fryer to reach 350º Fahrenheit.
2. Sprinkle the chops using pepper and salt.
3. Arrange the pork chops in the Air Fryer. Set the
   timer for 15 minutes.

4. Chop and sauté the mushrooms for 3 minutes and spritz with lemon juice.
5. Toss in the flour and herbs. Continue to sauté for about 4 minutes and set aside.
6. Prepare five sheets of foil for the chops. Arrange the chops on the foil and add some of the mushroom fixings.
7. Carefully fold the foil to seal in the chop and juices.
8. Add the chops in the fryer for 30 minutes.
9. Serve with a side salad.

Tandoori Chicken

Servings Provided: 4

Nutritional Facts Per Serving:

- **Protein Count**:25 grams
- **Net Carbohydrates**: 2 grams
- **Total Fat Content**: 6 grams
- **Calorie Count**: 178

Ingredients Needed:

- Greek yogurt (.25 cup)
- Chicken tenders (1 lb.)
- Fresh ginger (1 tbsp.)
- Garlic (1 tbsp.)
- Cilantro or parsley (.25 cup)
- Salt (1 tsp.)

- Cayenne pepper (.5-1 tsp.)
- Turmeric (1 tsp.)
- Garam masala (1 tsp.)
- Sweet smoked paprika (1 tsp.)
- *For Finishing*:
- Oil or ghee - for basting (1 tbsp.)
- Lemon juice (2 tsp.)
- Chopped cilantro (2 tbsp.)

Preparation Technique:

1. Cut each of the chicken tenders into halves. Mince the ginger and garlic.
2. Use a glass mixing container to mix each of the fixings except for the basting oil, lemon juice, and two tablespoons of the cilantro.
3. Set the timer for 25 minutes. At that time, turn on your Air Fryer to preheat to 350° Fahrenheit for 5 minutes.
4. After about 30 minutes, carefully lay the tandoori chicken in a single layer on the rack of the basket of the Air Fryer.
5. Baste the chicken using a silicone brush using the ghee or oil on one side. Air-fry for 10 minutes.
6. Remove the chicken and flip it over. Baste the other side. Cook for another 5 minutes. Using a meat thermometer, check to see if the internal temperature has reached 165° Fahrenheit. Do not skip this step.
7. Transfer it to a large bowl or platter. Spritz with the lemon juice and toss. Sprinkle with cilantro.

Whole Chicken: Rotisserie Style

Servings Provided: 4

Nutritional Facts Per Serving:

- **Protein Count**: 35 grams
- **Net Carbohydrates**: 0 grams
- **Total Fat Content**: 36 grams
- **Calorie Count**: 475

Ingredients Needed:

- Olive oil (2 tsp. or as needed)
- Whole chicken (6-7 lb.)
- Seasoned salt (1 tbsp.)

Preparation Technique:

1. Preheat the fryer at 350º Fahrenheit.
2. Clean and dry the chicken and coat with oil. Season with the salt.
3. Arrange the chicken in the Air Fryer – skin-side down.
4. Cook for 30 minutes. Flip the chicken over and air-fry for another 30 minutes.
5. Wait for ten minutes before slicing
6. Serve any way you like it.
7. Note: Under 6 lb. for a 3.7-quart Air Fryer

Desserts:

Butter Cake

Servings Provided: 8

Nutritional Facts Per Serving:

- **Protein Count**: 4 grams
- **Net Carbohydrates**: 0.8 grams
- **Total Fat Content**: 31 grams
- **Calorie Count**: 287

Ingredients Needed:

- Butter (1 cup)
- Liquid stevia (.25 cup)
- Pure vanilla extract (1 tbsp.)
- Almond flour (3 cups)
- Egg yolks (6) + Whole egg (1 large)
- Salt (.25 tsp.)
- Also Needed: 9-inch springform pan

Preparation Technique:

1. Warm the Air Fryer to reach 350º Fahrenheit.
2. Combine the stevia and butter using an electric hand mixer until creamy.
3. Gradually, mix in the yolks and vanilla.
4. Add to the pan, spreading the batter smoothly using a spatula.

5. Put the batter in the refrigerator and wait for about 15 minutes before cooking.
6. Whisk an egg and brush the cake. Air-fry for 35 minutes.

Delicious Blackberry Pie

Servings Provided: 8

Nutritional Facts Per Serving:

- **Protein Count**: 1.7 grams
- **Net Carbohydrates**: 1.6 grams
- **Total Fat Content**: 3.5 grams
- **Calorie Count**: 60

Ingredients Needed:

- Egg (1 large)
- Unsalted butter (2 tbsp.)
- Stevia (1 scoop)
- Baking powder (1 tbsp.)
- Almond flour (1 cup)
- Blackberries (.5 cup)
- Also Needed: Parchment paper

Preparation Technique:

1. Warm the Air Fryer to reach 350º Fahrenheit.
2. Whisk the egg, butter, stevia, and baking powder.
3. Reserve 1 teaspoon of the flour and add the rest to the mixture. Knead until smooth – not sticky.
4. Cover the fryer basket using a layer of baking paper and add the dough. Flatten into a pie

crust and add the berries. Sprinkle with the rest of the almond flour on top.
5. Air-fry until it's golden or about 20 minutes. Chill before slicing to serve.

Easy Cheesecake

Servings Provided: 6

Nutritional Facts Per Serving:

- **Protein Count**: 6.6 grams
- **Net Carbohydrates**: 2.6 grams
- **Total Fat Content**: 30.4 grams
- **Calorie Count**: 307

Ingredients Needed:

- Butter (6 tbsp.)
- Almonds (.5 cup)
- Stevia 1 tbsp.)
- Vanilla extract (.5 tsp.)
- Cream cheese (1 cup)
- Eggs (2)
- Swerve (2 tbsp.)
- Lemon zest (1 tsp.)
- Cinnamon (.25 tsp.)
- Also Needed: Parchment paper

Preparation Technique:

1. Combine the butter, vanilla, stevia, and sliced almonds.
2. Cover the Air Fryer tray with the paper and add the cheesecake crust.
3. Combine the cinnamon, swerve, lemon zest, and cream cheese.
4. Use a hand mixer to prepare the eggs until soft and fluffy. Pour the cream cheese mixture over the almond crust.
5. Set the Air Fryer at 310º Fahrenheit. Cook for 16 minutes. When it's done, chill for at least two hours.
6. Then, slice and serve.

Keto Chocolate Chip Cookies

Servings Provided: 5

Nutritional Facts Per Serving:

- **Protein Count**:3 grams
- **Net Carbohydrates**: 3.2 grams
- **Total Fat Content**: 15.2 grams
- **Calorie Count**: 157

Ingredients Needed:

- Dark chocolate chips (2 tbsp.)
- Egg (1)
- Salted butter (3 tbsp.)
- Crushed macadamia nuts (3 tbsp.)
- Almond flour (1 cup)

- Vanilla extract (.5 tsp.)
- Stevia (1 tsp.)
- Baking powder (.25 tsp.)
- Salt (.25 tsp.)

Preparation Technique:

1. Whisk the eggs and mix in with the flour and butter.
2. Stir in the rest of the fixings and knead the dough.
3. Make five balls for the cookie dough.
4. Heat the Air Fryer at 360º Fahrenheit.
5. Arrange the cookies in the fryer and flatten (lightly) and set the timer for 15 minutes.
6. Cool slightly and enjoy.

Lemon Cake

Servings Provided: 16

Nutritional Facts Per Serving:

- **Protein Count**: 1.5 grams
- **Net Carbohydrates**: 0.1 grams
- **Total Fat Content**: 27 grams
- **Calorie Count**: 231

Ingredients Needed:

- Sea salt (1 pinch)
- Warmed butter (2 cups)
- Liquid stevia (.25 cup)

- Large eggs (4)
- Baking powder (2 tbsp.)
- Almond flour (2 cups)
- Untreated & grated lemon rind (1)

Preparation Technique:

1. Heat the Air Fryer at 320º Fahrenheit.
2. Use a sheet of parchment baking paper to line a baking tray or use a coating of butter.
3. Warm the two cups of butter with the salt and stevia.
4. Zest the lemon and combine with the eggs, mixing until consistent and creamy.
5. Sift in the baking powder and flour. Empty the batter into the baking pan.
6. Air-fry for 35 minutes.

Rolled Cookies

Servings Provided: 8

Nutritional Facts Per Serving:

- **Protein Count**: 3 grams
- **Net Carbohydrates**: 0.5 grams
- **Total Fat Content**: 35 grams
- **Calorie Count**: 341

Ingredients Needed:

- Vanilla extract (1 tbsp.)
- Liquid stevia (4 tbsp.)

- Unchilled butter (1.5 cups)
- Large eggs (4)
- Almond flour (4 cups)
- Baking powder (2 tbsp.)
- Salt (1 tsp.)

Preparation Technique:

1. Cream the stevia and butter in a deep mixing dish.
2. Whisk and fold in the eggs and vanilla.
3. Stir in the baking powder, flour, and salt. Mix well and cover the batter container, and place it in the refrigerator for two hours to chill.
4. Warm the Air Fryer to reach 390º Fahrenheit.
5. Roll the dough until flat using a floured cutting board or another flat surface. Use a cookie cutter to make the cookie shapes.
6. Arrange the cookies in the fryer basket to cook for 10 minutes or until browned.
7. Cool and store.

Chapter 10: Tasty Vegan Air Fried Favorites

Each of these delicious vegan dishes also has the macros calculated if you're on the keto diet. They are all prepared for your dining delight!

Flax Egg

Servings Provided: 1

Nutritional Facts Per Serving:

- **Protein Count**: 1.1 grams
- **Net Carbohydrates**: 0.2 grams
- **Total Fat Content**: 2.7 grams
- **Calorie Count**: 37

Ingredients Needed:

- Ground flaxseed (1 tbsp.)
- Lukewarm water (2-3 tbsp.)

Preparation Technique:

1. Combine the ingredients in a mixing container.
2. Place a cover on the bowl and wait for ten minutes.
3. Use the mixture within five days kept in an airtight bowl or use immediately.
4. Replace one egg using this combination.

Breakfast:

Carrot Mix

Servings Provided: 4

Nutritional Facts Per Serving:

- **Protein Count**: 3 grams
- **Net Carbohydrates**: 4 grams
- **Total Fat Content**: 7 grams
- **Calorie Count**: 202

Ingredients Needed:

- Coconut milk (2 cups)
- Steel-cut oats (.5 cup)
- Shredded carrots (1 cup)
- Agave nectar (.5 tsp.)
- Ground cardamom (1 tsp.)
- Saffron (1 pinch)

Preparation Technique:

1. Lightly spritz the Air Fryer pan using a cooking oil spray.
2. Warm the fryer to reach 365º Fahrenheit.
3. When it's hot, whisk and add the fixings (omit the saffron).
4. Set the timer for 15 minutes.
5. After the timer buzzes, portion into the serving dishes with a sprinkle of saffron.

Chinese Breakfast Bowls

Servings Provided: 4

Nutritional Facts Per Serving:

- **Protein Count**: 3 grams
- **Net Carbohydrates**: 2 grams
- **Total Fat Content**: 5 grams
- **Calorie Count**: 159

Ingredients Needed:

- Firm tofu (12 oz.)
- Maple syrup (3 tbsp.)
- Coconut aminos (.25 cup)
- Sesame oil (2 tbsp.)
- Lime juice (2 tbsp.)
- Fresh romanesco (1 lb.)
- Carrots (3)
- Red bell pepper (1)
- Cooked red quinoa (2 cups)
- Torn spinach (8 oz.)

Preparation Technique:

1. Warm the Air Fryer at 370º Fahrenheit.
2. Cube the tofu and roughly chop the romanesco, carrots, and bell pepper.
3. Combine the juice, aminos, maple syrup, and oil with the tofu cubes in a mixing container.
4. Toss everything into the Air Fryer for 15 minutes. Shake the basket often.
5. Add the peppers, quinoa, spinach, carrots, and romanesco into serving dishes and enjoy.

Easy Breakfast Oats

Servings Provided: 4

Nutritional Facts Per Serving:

- **Protein Count**: 6 grams
- **Net Carbohydrates**: 5 grams
- **Total Fat Content**: 7 grams
- **Calorie Count**: 172

Ingredients Needed:

- Almond milk (2 cups)
- Steel-cut oats (1 cup)
- Water (2 cups)
- Dried cherries (.33 cup)
- Cocoa powder (2 tbsp.)
- Stevia (.25 cup)
- Almond extract (.5 tsp.)
- *The Sauce:*
- Water (2 tbsp.)
- Cherries (1.5 cups)
- Almond extract (.25 tsp.)

Preparation Technique:

1. Warm the fryer to reach 360º Fahrenheit.
2. Stir the first set of ingredients into the pan of the Air Fryer. Set the timer for 15 minutes.
3. In a small pot, whisk the sauce fixings. Simmer for 10 minutes.
4. Portion into serving bowls with a drizzle of the cherry sauce.

Pumpkin Oatmeal

Servings Provided: 4

Nutritional Facts Per Serving:

- **Protein Count**: 3 grams
- **Net Carbohydrates**:1 gram
- **Total Fat Content**: 4 grams
- **Calorie Count**: 211

Ingredients Needed:

- Water (1.5 cups)
- Pumpkin puree (.5 cup)
- Stevia (3 tbsp.)
- Pumpkin pie spice (1 tsp.)
- Steel-cut oats (.5 cup)

Preparation Technique:

1. Set the Air Fryer at 360º Fahrenheit to preheat.
2. Toss in and mix the fixings into the pan of the Air Fryer.
3. Set the timer for 20 minutes.
4. When the time has elapsed, portion the oatmeal into bowls and serve.

Lunch:

Carrot & Potato Mix

Servings Provided: 6

Nutritional Facts Per Serving:

- **Protein Count**: 4 grams
- **Net Carbohydrates**: 1 gram
- **Total Fat Content**: 4 grams
- **Calorie Count**: 241

Ingredients Needed:

- Potatoes (2)
- Carrots (3 lb.)
- Yellow onion (1)
- Dried thyme (1 tsp.)
- Black pepper and salt (to your liking)
- Curry powder (2 tsp.)
- Coconut milk (3 tbsp.)
- Vegan cheese (3 tbsp.)
- Parsley (1 tbsp.)

Preparation Technique:

1. Cube/chop the parsley, carrots, and onions. Crumble the vegan cheese.
2. Warm the Air Fryer to reach 365° Fahrenheit.

3. Once it's heated, toss in the veggies, thyme, curry powder, salt, and pepper. Set the timer and air-fry for 16 minutes.
4. Stir in the milk and cheese.
5. Portion and serve.

Curried Cauliflower Florets With Nuts & Raisins

Servings Provided: 4

Nutritional Facts Per Serving:

- **Protein Count**: 9.5 grams
- **Net Carbohydrates**: 8.6 grams
- **Total Fat Content**: 11.3 grams
- **Calorie Count**: 275

Ingredients Needed:

- Golden raisins (.25 cup)
- Cauliflower (1 head)
- Pine nuts (.25 cup)
- Boiling water (1 cup)
- Olive oil (.5 cup)
- Curry powder (1 tbsp.)
- Salt (.25 tsp.)

Preparation Technique:

1. Slice the cauliflower into small florets.
2. Dump the raisins into the cup of boiling water to plump.
3. Set the Air Fryer temperature at 350º Fahrenheit.
4. Toast the nuts in the fryer with the oil for about one minute.
5. Toss the florets with the salt and curry powder in another mixing bowl. Toss into the Air Fryer.
6. Cook for ten minutes. Drain and toss all of the fixings well before serving.

Falafel - Gluten-Free

Servings Provided: 4 - 3 each - 12 patties

Nutritional Facts Per Serving:

- **Protein Count**: 11.5 grams
- **Net Carbohydrates**: 5.1 grams
- **Total Fat Content**: 12.2 grams
- **Calorie Count**: 188

Ingredients Needed:

- Brined lupini beans (1 cup)
- Thawed - frozen broccoli (1.5 cups)
- Tahini (.25 cup)
- Lemon juice (2 tbsp.)
- Dried parsley (1 tbsp.)
- Cumin (2 tsp.)
- Ground chia seeds (2 tbsp.)
- Garlic powder (.5 tsp.)
- Onion powder (.25 tsp.)

- Allspice (.25 tsp.)

Preparation Technique:

1. Before you begin, soak the lupini beans in hot water (30-60 min.) and drain them.
2. Warm the fryer to 350° Fahrenheit.
3. Chop the broccoli and beans using a food processor until they are in rice-like pieces. Transfer this mixture to a medium-sized mixing container.
4. Add the lemon juice, tahini, and seasoning to the mixture and stir until combined.
5. Stir in the ground chia seeds. Wait for the mixture to sit for about 5 minutes, so the chia can absorb some liquid to make a thick dough form.
6. Shape the dough mixture into 12 patties, and then flattened them to be about 2 inches across and a little less than ½-inch thick.
7. Arrange the patties in a single layer in the Air Fryer and air-fry for 14-15 minutes, depending on how crunchy you like them.
8. Serve while warm.
9. To Reheat: Air-fry for 8 minutes at 350° Fahrenheit.

Roasted Asian Broccoli

Servings Provided: 4 sides

Nutritional Facts Per Serving:

- **Protein Count**: 6.4 grams
- **Net Carbohydrates**: 6.7 grams
- **Total Fat Content**: 10.8 grams
- **Calorie Count**: 154

Ingredients Needed:

- Broccoli (1 lb.)
- Peanut oil (1.5 tbsp.)
- Garlic (1 tbsp.)
- Salt
- Reduced sodium soy sauce (2 tbsp.)
- Honey (or agave (2 tsp.)
- Sriracha (2 tsp.)
- Rice vinegar (1 tsp.)
- Roasted salted peanuts (.33 cup)
- Optional: Fresh lime juice

Preparation Technique:

1. Warm the Air Fryer to reach 400° Fahrenheit.
2. Mince the garlic. Slice the broccoli into florets.
3. Toss the broccoli, peanut oil, garlic, and sea salt until well covered.
4. Arrange the broccoli in the wire basket of the Air Fryer, trying to leave a little bit of space between each of the florets.
5. Cook until golden brown and crispy (15-20 min.), stirring halfway.
6. Mix the honey, soy sauce, sriracha, and rice vinegar in a small, microwave-safe bowl.

7. Once well mixed, microwave the mixture for 10-15 seconds until the honey is melted and evenly incorporated.
8. Toss the broccoli into a bowl and add in the soy sauce mixture.
9. Toss to coat and season to taste with a pinch more salt, if needed. Stir in the peanuts and squeeze a drizzle of lime on top as desired.

Yellow Squash - Carrots & Zucchini

Servings Provided: 4

Nutritional Facts Per Serving:

- **Protein Count**:7.4 grams
- **Net Carbohydrates**: 8.6 grams
- **Total Fat Content**: 9.4 grams
- **Calorie Count**: 256

Ingredients Needed:

- Carrots (.5 lb.)
- Olive oil (6 tsp. - divided)
- Lime (1 sliced into wedges)
- Zucchini (1 lb. sliced into .75-inch semi-circles)
- Yellow squash (1 lb.)
- Tarragon leaves (1 tbsp.)
- White pepper (.5 tsp.)
- Sea salt (1 tsp.)

Preparation Technique:

1. Set the Air Fryer at 400º Fahrenheit.
2. Trim the stem and roots from the squash and
    zucchini.
3. Dice and add the carrots into a bowl with two
    teaspoons of oil.
4. Toss the carrots into the fryer basket. Prepare
    for 5 minutes.
5. Mix in the zucchini, oil, salt, and pepper in the
    bowl.
6. When the carrots are done, fold in the mixture.
    Cook 30 minutes.
7. Stir the mixture occasionally. Chop the tarragon
    and garnish using and lime wedges.

Dinner:

Mexican Casserole

Servings Provided: 4

Nutritional Facts Per Serving:

- **Protein Count**: 8 grams
- **Net Carbohydrates**:3 grams
- **Total Fat Content**: 5 grams
- **Calorie Count**: 223

Ingredients Needed:

- Olive oil (1 tbsp.)
- Garlic (4 cloves)
- Onion (1 yellow)
- Cilantro (2 tbsp.)
- Red chili (1 small)
- Ground cumin (2 tsp.)
- Coriander seeds (1 tsp.)
- Sweet paprika (1 tsp.)
- Black pepper and salt (as desired)
- Sweet potatoes (1 lb.)
- Lime juice (half of 1 lime)
- Green beans (10 oz.)
- Tomatoes (2 cups)
- Parsley (1 tbsp.)

Preparation Technique:

1. Set the Air Fryer at 365º Fahrenheit.
2. Mince or chop the garlic, onions, red chili, tomatoes, parsley, and cilantro. Cube the sweet potatoes.
3. Spritz a pan to fit inside of the Air Fryer using a bit of cooking oil spray.
4. Mix and add all of the fixings (omitting the parsley for now).
5. Set the timer for 15 minutes. Add parsley to the casserole and serve.

Rice & Endive Casserole

Servings Provided: 4

Nutritional Facts Per Serving:

- **Protein Count**: 6 grams
- **Net Carbohydrates**: 4 grams
- **Total Fat Content**: 5 grams
- **Calorie Count**: 220

Ingredients Needed:

- Olive oil (1 tbsp.)
- Scallions (2)
- Garlic (3 cloves)
- Fresh ginger (1 tbsp.)
- Chili sauce (1 tsp.)
- White/brown rice (.5 cup)
- Veggie stock (1 cup)
- Endives (3)
- Black pepper and salt (1 pinch)

Preparation Technique:

1. Chop/grate the garlic, scallions, trimmed endives, and ginger.
2. Lightly grease a pan that will fit in the Air Fryer using a spritz of oil.
3. Mix all of the fixings in the fryer and set the timer for 20 minutes.
4. When it's ready, divide into plates and serve.

Delicious Mix & Match Side Dishes

Baby Ears Of Corn

Servings Provided: 4

Nutritional Facts Per Serving:

- **Protein Count**: 10.3 grams
- **Net Carbohydrates**: 8.2 grams
- **Total Fat Content**: 9.6 grams
- **Calorie Count**: 243

Ingredients Needed:

- Carom seeds (.5 tsp.)
- Almond flour (1 cup)
- Chili powder (.25 tsp.)
- Garlic powder (1 tsp.)
- Boiled baby ears of corn (4)
- Baking soda (1 pinch)
- Salt (to your liking)

Preparation Technique:

1. Warm the Air Fryer (350º Fahrenheit).
2. Whisk the flour, salt, carom seeds, baking soda, garlic powder, and chili powder.
3. Pour in a little water to make a batter. Dip the boiled corn in the mixture.

4. Place the corn in a foil-lined fryer basket. Air-fry
   10 minutes.
5. Serve with a sprinkle of salt if desired.

Crunchy Black-Eyed Peas

Servings Provided: 6

Nutritional Facts Per Serving:

- **Protein Count**: 9.2 grams
- **Net Carbohydrates**: 8.6 grams
- **Total Fat Content**: 9.4 grams
- **Calorie Count**: 262

Ingredients Needed:

- Black-eyed peas (15 oz. can)
- Salt (.25 tsp.)
- Chipotle chili powder (.125 tsp.)
- Black pepper (.125 tsp.)
- Chili powder (.5 tsp.)

Preparation Technique:

1. Use cold tap water to rinse the beans. Set aside
   for now.
2. Set the Air Fryer temperature at 360°
   Fahrenheit.
3. Whisk the spices and add the peas.
4. Add to the fryer basket and air-fry for 10
   minutes.

Easy Tofu

Servings Provided: 4

Nutritional Facts Per Serving:

- **Protein Count**: 7 grams
- **Net Carbohydrates**:4 grams
- **Total Fat Content**: 5.6 grams
- **Calorie Count**: 89.5

Ingredients Needed:

- Sesame oil (2 tbsp.)
- Cornstarch (1 tbsp.)
- Tofu (1 block/1-inch cubes)
- Rice vinegar (1 tsp.)
- Tamari/Coconut Aminos/keto-friendly substitute for soy sauce (2 tbsp.)

Preparation Technique:

1. Warm up the fryer ahead of time to 370º Fahrenheit.
2. Combine the oil, vinegar, tofu, and tamari/aminos. Toss well and set aside.
3. Toss the cornstarch in a dish and cover the tofu.
4. Place it in the Air Fryer basket for 20 minutes. Toss the tofu a couple of times during the air-fry cycle.

Lemony Green Beans

Servings Provided: 4

Nutritional Facts Per Serving:

- **Protein Count**: 8.7 grams
- **Net Carbohydrates**: 8.6 grams
- **Total Fat Content**: 9.2 grams
- **Calorie Count**: 263

Ingredients Needed:

- Lemon (1)
- Green beans (1 lb.)
- Extra-virgin olive oil (.25 tsp.)
- Black pepper & sea salt (as desired

Preparation Technique:

1. Set the Air Fryer temperature setting at 400º Fahrenheit.
2. Pour the beans into the fryer basket, and spritz using the lemon juice, oil, salt, and pepper.
3. Air-fry for 12 minutes. Serve immediately.

Tawa Vegetables

Servings Provided: 4

Nutritional Facts Per Serving:

- **Protein Count**: 8.7 grams
- **Net Carbohydrates**: 10.4 grams
- **Total Fat Content**: 11.3 grams
- **Calorie Count**: 264

Ingredients Needed:

- Potato (.25 cup)
- Okra (.25 cup)
- Taro root (.25 cup)
- Eggplant (.25 cup)
- Garam masala (2 tsp.)
- Red chili powder (1 tsp.)
- Amchur powder (1 tsp.)
- Salt (as desired)
- For Brushing: Olive oil

Preparation Technique:

1. Set the Air Fryer at 390º Fahrenheit.
2. Slice the taro root and potatoes into fries and soak them in salted water for ten minutes.
3. Slice the eggplant and okra into four sections.
4. Rinse the potatoes and taro root; pat dry. Combine with the spices, okra, and eggplant.
5. Brush the pan with the oil and air-fry for 10 minutes. Lower the heat setting to 355º Fahrenheit and cook 15 additional minutes.
6. Enjoy them any way you choose.

Desserts:

Apple Chips

Servings Provided: 2

Nutritional Facts Per Serving:

- **Net Carbohydrates**:10 grams
- **Calorie Count**: 48

Ingredients Needed:

- Apple (1 large thinly sliced)
- Cinnamon (1 tsp.)
- Salt (1 pinch)
- Avocado/olive oil spray (1 tsp.)

Preparation Technique:

1. Warm the Air Fryer to 350º Fahrenheit.
2. Use a mandolin or sharp knife to slice the apples.
3. Toss them into a container with the salt and cinnamon. Toss well. Lightly spritz with oil as needed.
4. Arrange them in the fryer basket - not touching.
5. Set the timer for 8 to 10 minutes. Flatten them a couple of times while cooking.
6. Remove the batch and repeat until the rest of the slices are air-fried.

Blueberry Smoothie

Servings Provided: 1

Nutritional Facts Per Serving:

- **Protein Count**: 23 grams
- **Net Carbohydrates**: 4 grams
- **Total Fat Content**:10 grams
- **Calorie Count**: 215

Ingredients Needed:

- Coconut/almond milk (1 cup)
- Blueberries (.25 cup)
- Vanilla extract (1 tsp.)
- MCT Oil/more coconut oil (1 tsp.)
- Optional: Protein powder/your choice (30 grams)

Preparation Technique:

1. Toss each of the fixings into a blender.
2. Mix well and serve in a chilled glass.

Clean & Green Smoothie

Servings Provided: 1 or 1.5 cups

Nutritional Facts Per Serving:

- **Protein Count**:10 grams
- **Net Carbohydrates**: 4 grams
- **Total Fat Content**: 33 grams

- **Calorie Count**: 360

Ingredients Needed:

- Filtered water (1 cup)
- Avocado (half of 1)
- MCT oil (1 tbsp.)
- Organic cucumber (half of 1)
- Dark leafy greens (1 large handful)
- Dandelion (1 – 2 leaves)
- Parsley (2 tbsp.)
- Hemp seeds (2 tbsp.)
- Lemon juice (1 lemon)
- Turmeric powder (.25 tsp.)

Preparation Technique:

1. Toss each of the components into a high-speed blender.
2. Pulse the smoothie about one minute.
3. Serve and enjoy immediately.

Frozen Berry Shake

Servings Provided: 1

Nutritional Facts Per Serving:

- **Protein Count**: 4 grams
- **Net Carbohydrates**: 6.7 grams
- **Total Fat Content**: 41 grams
- **Calorie Count**: 400

Ingredients Needed:

- Frozen mixed berries (.5 cup)
- Creamed coconut milk (.33 cup)
- MCT/Virgin coconut oil (1 tbsp.)
- Water/unsweetened almond milk (.5 cup)
- Optional: Stevia extract (3-5 drops)

Preparation Technique:

1. Cream the coconut milk by placing the can in the fridge overnight. The next day, open and spoon out the solidified coconut milk and discard the liquids. *Don't shake* before opening the can. (One 400 gram container yields about 200 grams of coconut cream.)
2. Place the creamed coconut milk, berries, water/almond milk, MCT oil, and stevia (if using) and ice into a blender.
3. Pulse until smooth.

Green Avocado Pudding

Servings Provided: 3

Nutritional Facts Per Serving:

- **Protein Count**: 2.2 grams
- **Net Carbohydrates**: 2.6 grams
- **Total Fat Content**: 19.3 grams
- **Calorie Count**: 199

Ingredients Needed:

- Pitted avocado (1)

- Almond milk (5 tbsp.)
- Stevia (3 tsp.)
- Vanilla extract (.25 tsp.)
- Salt (.25 tsp.)
- Cocoa powder (1 tbsp.)

Preparation Technique:

1. Set the Air Fryer at 360° Fahrenheit.
2. Peel and mash the avocad. Mix it with the milk, salt, vanilla extract, and stevia. Stir in the cocoa powder.
3. Cook the pudding in the Air Fryer for three minutes.
4. Chill and serve.

Index For The Recipes:

Chapter 1: Brunch Specialties

- Air Fryer Bacon
- Air Fryer Bagels
- Apple Dumplings
- Avocado Egg Boats
- Baked Apple & Walnuts
- Baked Eggs In A Bread Bowl
- Banana Fritters
- Cheesy Mushroom Onion Frittata
- Chicken Breakfast Burrito
- Chocolate & Avocado Muffins
- Churros
- Delicious Doughnuts In A Jiffy
- French Toast Soldiers
- Ham - Egg - Mushroom & Cheese Croissant
- Ham Hash
- Loaded Hash Browns
- Pepperoni - Egg & Cheese Pizza
- Quick & Easy Poached Eggs
- Sausage Wraps
- Scrambled Eggs
- Sweet Potato Hash
- Western Omelet

Delicious Bread Options

- Bread Rolls With Potato Stuffing

- Cheesy Garlic Bread

Chapter 2: Lunch Favorites

- Bourbon Bacon Burger
- Cheeseburger 'Mini' Sliders
- Chicken Fried Rice
- Egg Rolls
- Fried Tortellini
- Grilled Cheese Sandwiches
- Hawaiian Pizzas
- Loaded Twice Baked Air-Fried Potatoes
- Luncheon Tacos
- Mac N Cheese Balls
- Pigs In A Blanket
- Pita Bread Pizza - Pepperoni Sausage & Onion
- Pizza Dogs
- Portobello Stuffed Mushrooms
- Ravioli
- Reuben Roasted Turkey Sandwiches
- Roasted Veggie Pasta Salad
- Simple Hot Dogs & Cheese
- Weight Watchers Mozzarella Cheese Sticks

Chapter 3: Seafood & Fish Choices

- Black Cod With Fennel, Kale, Pecans & Grapes
- Breaded Cod Sticks
- Cajun Salmon
- Cajun Shrimp

- Clams Oregano
- Coconut Shrimp
- Crispy Halibut
- Fish & Chips
- Fried Catfish
- Ginger Cod Steaks
- Quick & Easy Crab Sticks
- Salmon Patties
- Sriracha & Honey Tossed Calamari
- Teriyaki Glazed Halibut Steak

Chapter 4: Poultry Options

- BBQ Chicken - Gluten-Free
- Buffalo Chicken Wings
- Chicken Breast Tenderloins
- Chicken Curry
- Chicken Fillet Strips
- Chicken Kabobs
- Chicken Pot Pie
- Crispy Chicken Sliders
- Fried Chicken Thighs
- Garlic Herb Turkey Breast
- Mustard-Glazed Turkey Breast
- Parmesan Chicken
- Philly Chicken Cheese Steak Stromboli

Chapter 5: Pork & Lamb Favorites

Pork

- Bacon-Wrapped Pork Tenderloin
- Crispy Breaded Pork Chops
- Pork Meatballs
- Pork Taquitos
- Ranch Pork Chops
- Roast Pork Loin With Red Potatoes
- Smoked Balsamic Raspberry Pork Chops
- Southern Fried Chops

Lamb

- Lamb Ribs - Saltimbocca
- Lamb & Turkey Meatballs
- Macadamia Crusted Roasted Rack Of Lamb
- Spicy Lamb Sirloin

Chapter 6: Beef & Dinner Time Variety Options

Beef

- Air Fried Beef & Potato
- Beef Empanadas
- Beef & Bacon Taco Rolls
- Beef Stew

- Black Peppercorns Meatloaf
- Breaded Beef Schnitzel
- Cheesy Beef Enchiladas
- Country Fried Steak
- Easy Rib Steak
- Inside Out Cheeseburgers
- Mongolian Beef
- Roast Beef
- Steak & Mushrooms

Other Dinners

- Bratwurst & Veggies
- Stromboli

Chapter 7: Side Dishes & Appetizers

- Air-Fried Okra
- Avocado & Bacon Fries
- Battered Baby Ears Of Corn
- Breaded Avocado Fries
- Brussels Sprouts
- Buffalo Cauliflower
- Buttery Blossoming Onions
- Charred Shishito Peppers
- Crispy Onion Rings
- Cumin Butternut Squash
- Hasselback Potatoes
- Honey Roasted Carrots
- Mediterranean Veggies
- Mushroom Melt
- Potato Hay

- Semolina Veggie Cutlets
- Smoked Cheese Asparagus
- Sour Cream Stuffed Mushrooms
- Sweet Potato Tots
- Thyme & Garlic Tomatoes

Chapter 8: Desserts Galore

- Air Fried Plantains
- Air Fryer Beignets
- Banana Smores
- Blackberry & Apricot Crumble
- Blueberry Hand Pies
- Brownies
- Caramel Cream-Dipped Apple Fries
- Cheesecake Egg Rolls
- Cherry Pie
- Chocolate Cake
- Cinnamon Rolls
- Donut Bread Pudding
- Guilt-Free Paleo Pumpkin Muffins
- Iced Strawberry Cupcakes
- Molten Lava Cakes
- Smores
- Yam & Marshmallow Hand Pies

Chapter 9: Delicious Ketogenic Air Fried Specialties

Breakfast

- Air Bread & Egg Butter
- Asparagus Omelet
- Bacon Egg & Cheese Roll-Ups
- Brunch Ham Hash
- Dark Chocolate Avocado Muffins
- Eggs - Ham & Spinach
- Pumpkin Pie French Toast
- Scrambled Pancake Hash
- Thai Omelet
- Tofu Egg Muffins
- Turkey "Sausage" Patties

Lunch

- Bacon-Wrapped Chicken
- Beef Roll-Ups
- Chicken Hash
- Dragon Shrimp
- Fish Nuggets
- Roast Beef For Sandwiches
- Turkey & Avocado Burrito

Dinner

- Chicken Strips
- Creamy Salmon

- Shrimp Scampi
- Stuffed Pork Chops
- Tandoori Chicken
- Whole Chicken: Rotisserie Style

Desserts

- Butter Cake
- Delicious Blackberry Pie
- Easy Cheesecake
- Keto Chocolate Chip Cookies
- Lemon Cake
- Rolled Cookies

Chapter 10: Tasty Vegan Air Fried Favorites

- Flax Egg

Breakfast:

- Carrot Mix
- Chinese Breakfast Bowls
- Easy Breakfast Oats
- Pumpkin Oatmeal

Lunch

- Carrot & Potato Mix
- Curried Cauliflower Florets With Nuts & Raisins
- Falafel - Gluten-Free
- Roasted Asian Broccoli
- Yellow Squash - Carrots & Zucchini

Dinner

- Mexican Casserole
- Rice & Endive Casserole

Delicious Mix & Match Side Dishes

- Baby Ears Of Corn
- Crunchy Black-Eyed Peas
- Easy Tofu
- Lemony Green Beans
- Tawa Vegetables

Desserts:

- Apple Chips
- Blueberry Smoothie
- Clean & Green Smoothie
- Frozen Berry Shake
- Green Avocado Pudding

Conclusion

You will discover all of the reasons you will enjoy these delicious recipes once you know how convenient and energy-efficient meal planning is when you own an Air Fryer. The ability to grill, bake, and fry will make the Air Fryer a 'must-have' for any kitchen.

There's no recommendation for the amount of oil you need to add (unless shown in the recipes given). It will depend significantly on the types of food and your taste. You may cook many items without oil.

If you are vegan or are on the keto diet, you now see how easy it can be to measure out the ingredients and follow the step-by-step information provided for each of the tasty recipes that will keep you in the state of ketosis. All you need to do is gather a shopping list of what you need to become ketogenic and head to the superstore for supplies.

The meal combinations are flexible, and you will soon discover what you have been missing out of life with so much less time consumed in food prep. You know this is an excellent addition to your cookbook resources. It will surely be frequently used as you plan your weekly meal plans.

For Quick Reference Use This Chart:

You will find this chart convenient as you start using our Air Fryer since the US and Metric measurements do vary.

Metric Concersions & Equivalents:

LIQUID

US	METRIC
1 tsp	5 ml
1 tbs	15 ml
2 tbs	30 ml
1/4 cup	60 ml
1/3 cup	75 ml
1/2 cup	120 ml
2/3 cup	150 ml
3/4 cup	180 ml
1 cup	240 ml
1 1/4 cups	300 ml
1 1/3 cups	325 ml
1 1/2 cups	350 ml
1 2/3 cups	375 ml
1 3/4 cups	400 ml
2 cups (1 pint)	475 ml
3 cups	720 ml
4 cups (1 quart)	945 ml

LENGTH

US	METRIC
1/2 inch	1.25 cm
1 inch	2.5 cm
6 inches	15 cm
8 inches	20 cm
10 inches	25 cm
12 inches	30 cm

GENERAL METRIC CONVERSION FORMULAS

Ounces to grams	ounces x 28.35 = grams
Grams to ounces	grams x 0.035 = ounces
Pounds to grams	pounds x 435.5 = grams
Pounds to kilograms	pounds x 0.45 = kilograms
Cups to liters	cups x 0.24 = liters
Fahrenheit to Celsius	(°F - 32) x 5 ÷ 9 = °C
Celsius to Fahrenheit	(°C x 9) ÷ 5 + 32 = °F

WEIGHT

US	METRIC
1/2 oz	14 g
1 oz	28 g
1 1/2 oz	43 g
2 oz	57 g
2 1/2 oz	71 g
4 oz	113 g
5 oz	142 g
6 oz	170 g
7 oz	200 g
8 oz (1/2 lb)	227 g
9 oz	255 g
10 oz	264 g
11 oz	312 g
12 oz	340 g
13 oz	368 g
14 oz	400 g
15 oz	425 g
16 oz (1 lb)	454 g

OVEN TEMPERATURE

°F	Gas Mark	°C
250	1/2	120
275	1	140
300	2	150
325	3	165
350	4	180
375	5	190
400	6	200
425	7	220
450	8	230
475	9	240
500	10	260
550	Broil	290

www.ingramcontent.com/pod-product-compliance
Lightning Source LLC
Chambersburg PA
CBHW071401150726
48000CB00001B/119